Library Buildings and Furniture : Design and Planning

By

S.C. Sinha
M.A. Sociology (Lko, Univ.)
M.Lib. Sc. (Delhi Univ.)
Associateship in Information Science (INSDOC, Delhi)
Former Library Officer E.I. (CBRI, Roorkee)

Ess Ess Publications
4837/24, Ansari Road, Darya Ganj,
New Delhi-110002
✆ : 23260807
Fax : 23274173
E-mail: info@essessreference.com

First Published 2004

ISBN : 81-7000-381-4

Price : Rs. 375/-

Published by :
Ess Ess Publications
4837/24, Ansari Road, Darya Ganj,
New Delhi - 110 002
Phone : 23260807
Fax : 23274173
E-mail : essess@del3.vsnl.net.in

Printed at :
Print Line

Contents

Introduction

The library is a backbone of any organisation whether it is a public library, school library, college library, university library or a research Library. Inspite of the fact that however rich the collection of these libraries might be they would not fulfill their propose if their library buildings are not attractive with beautiful elevation and equipped with comfortable furniture only then would they attract readers and invite them to enter in these temples of knowledge and get enriched with mental food without any tension. The time spent in these libraries by the readers should be considered as the best utilised of their hours in these libraries. It is indeed very essential that such libraries must have an attractive buildings fully equipped with ultramodern furniture and have the useful holdings in the form of books, periodicals, non book material and should be fully equipped with electronic gadgets including computers helping the readers to get the desired information to a great extent and fulfill the intellectual needs of the readers so that they may tend to feel free from any tension as they use the library. The public libraries like The British Council Library, American Information Center Library, Delhi attract a big crowd of readers particularly in summers and winter vacations, the reason being few readers can afford this type of comfort in their houses. In foreign countries, people right from tiny tots to the elderly person visit their public libraries to pass their leisure time peacefully and gainfully.

From the above it is amply clear that the two very important components are Library Buildings and Furniture. These are vital components with thermal comfort facilities. The bad design of library buildings and uncomfortable library furniture can mar the very spirit of such libraries, therefore, the full attention must be paid while planning a new library building apart from their rich holdings.

In the present book efforts are made to provide complete knowledge of the subject in a simple techniques lucid style by avoiding the jargons used in science. Public Libraries are the primary institutions which might help in cultivating the reading habits amongst the young generation. In this context it will not be out of place to mention that these libraries must have grand attractive buildings with comfortable furniture and internet facilities and should be equipped with the electronics viz. Computers with audio-visual facilities, so that readers enrich themselves with latest information. Next come school, college and university libraries which provide them complete information to make the budding young fully equipped and educated young future citizens of a country on whose shoulders the future of the country lies.

Special Libraries sharpen the professional skills of those who consult them, these libraries must have attractive and comfortable buildings along with comfortable furniture so that they may use the library without any mental stress.

S.C. Sinha

Preface

Very few books of Indian authors are available in the market on Library Buildings and Design. Dr. P.N. Kaula's book on Library Building and Design was the first book that was written in 70's and another book by Dr. H. D. Sharma's in 96. The books written by foreign authors do not suit to our environment and needs.

I had a chance to visit a few foreign libraries and I worked in some of these libraries as an ITEC EXPERT (Library) for example, the Somali National University, Mogadishu, (Somalia) when I was deputed by Govt. of India. Recently I was in Ottawa, the capital of Canada where I visited few Public Libraries and University Libraries, inNepal I took the opportunity to visit Tribhuvan University Library, Kathmandu. I served as head of the library, Central Building Research Institute, Roorkee for more than 30 years and came in contact with Architecture & Physical Planning Division of the institute where the Physical planning division of the institute prepared drawings of the schools and Navovidayalas.

The book is divided into three parts. The first part deals with principles of architecture concerning library architecture and buildings. In this modern age of computers and automation, the design of buildings have undergone some changes. Part two deals the various types of library buildings and includes the case studies of few library buildings. Part three deals with various kinds of furniture with which the libraries should be equipped. The elevation plan and thermal comfort of library buildings add to the beauty and utility of the Libraries.

The book also covers the syllabi of Indian Universities which are running the post Graduate Courses in Library & Information Science and the students pursuing these courses will be amply benefitted.

I am thankful to many librarians who took trouble in showing me their libraries during my visit and discussing the strong and weak points of the library building and furniture. I am specially thankful to Shri Senapati of CBRI Library, Shri Yogendra Singh, Librarian, Central Library, IIT, Roorkee, Mohd. Furquan Ullah of NIH Library, who has recently shifted to the new circular type Library Building at NIH, Roorkee and the librarians of British Council and The American Information Center, Delhi.

In the end, I appreciate the management of my publisher M/s. Ess Ess Publications, Delhi in general and Shri Sumit Sethi and Mrs. S. Sethi in particular who have made genuine efforts to bring out this book in an attractive manner and I am closely associated with them as I could publish more than six books within a short span of three years. I am grateful to them. In the end I must thank my beloved wife Ms. Pratibha Sinha who remained a constant source of encouragement to allow me to steal her time while writing this book. My son Sumit, his wife Ms. Garima and my daughter Ms. Shruti Sinha who have always appreciated my efforts and encouraged me. I am thankful to Peter Prachar of Canada who encouraged me to visit the 'Public Library of Ottawa' and the 'University Library of Ottawa.'

S. C. Sinha

1

State of the Art of Library Buildings Physical Planing of Library Buildings; In European Countries

When man first collected knowledge in recorded form it became necessary to have a storage facility such that the recorded knowledge would be preserved but could be recalled with minimum efforts. Thus, the library building form has always been determined by the nature of stored materials, whether clay tablets, scrolls, books, films of tapes. The form of plan of the building most generally follows from this storage and retrieval function.

The British librarian, Anthony Thompson, has identified a variety of historic plans typing his "Library buildings of Britan and Europe (London, 1996). The " Classical Library Building was at Ephesus (A D 107) ; at first, these libraries were generally connected with temples, later they were attached to or were integral parts cathedrals and princely dwellings. The classical plan has continued into modern ties in such library buildings as those of Boston athenaeum (1855), the pebody Library in Baltimore (1861), and the parent office (1902) , and science Museum (1905) Libraries in London. The " medieval Plan " calls for a simple, one-room library ; it developed through several stages in a series of alcoves created by book shelves be with tables and chairs in each alcove. Very functional for small libraries or even for special collections or rooms within large libraries, in recent library for undergraduate students at Harvard University.

The real impetus to planning modern library buildings stemmed, according to Thompson, were from designs to to solve "the problem of issuing many books to many readers viz dissemination of information in modern terms. Three principal types of libraries on modern lines are identified: closed-bookstack, open-access, and various shaped: each of these have several sub-types. The first "modern" library building was the Bibliotheque Sainte-Genevieve at the University de Paris (6 1843) ; it is the prototype of all closed-stack libraries with reading a room above book-stacks below; although it solved the problem of having books and readers in close proximity, yet copied, most recently in the National Library of Medicine at Bethesda? Maryland (1962) ; A similar arrangement is that of readers' spaces in front with the book stacks behind.

Open access library buildings plans were a result of efforts in modern times to bring books and readers together. They developed first in public libraries, mainly from the stimulus of the many millions of dollars contributed to public library building by Andrew Carnegie. Latter, college and university Libraries opened their collection to students better open-access plans. Thompson cites the single-room plan and Carnegie rectangle "as developing into the right/ left plan, and later into the H. U. L, and V shaped building plans. The right/ left plan simply, is the single-room rectangular plan divided into rooms by aloin or control desk in the middle which supervises the two halves as well as entrance to the buildings. The right/ left plan is common today in small branch libraries buildingswere divided vertically with lending on the ground of entrance level and reference on a second floor where the quieter surroundings were more conducive to study in depth subject departmentalization as a plan for buildings was developed in public library of Leninggrad as early as in 1833, and in university library buildings in the late 1930's An example of the latter is the University of Colaroda Library (1940)

Finally, there are other shapes among these are the square, the circle, the triangle , the T shaped and the hollow or ring plan with a centeral coutyard. Interesting examples of the last mentioned types are Oarles Hayden Memorial Library, MIT with its central coutyard open to the exterior, and the Francis A. Country way Library, of Medicine at Harvard with its closed inter integrity, but at the cost of complicated interior traffic patters and a considerable waste of layout , the square-type plan is less costly since it has the least amount of exterior wall construction ; these types or plans listed by Thompson are helpful in identifying basic and single forms but , in practice, many library buildings incorporated several of the types. The countryard or light-wall can be fitted to most types and is very often today. Subject departmentalisation has been used in several of the types of the plan. An interesting plan is that proposed for the new libraries of the University of Masassachusetts at Amherest, which utilised the tower plan for bringing togather books and readers, rather than separating them as in the tower at the University of Rochester.

The rapidly expending book collections of the 20th century, the introduction of new electronic media (e.g. Microfilms, phonographs records, computerized storage media, computers its itself etc.) change in library services patterns, increased library staff and increasing library and information collectionshave caused greater attention to the function aspects of library buildings. Construction techniques of this and next century were applied to the advantage and through the efforts of many minds (particular through Angus snead mac Donald, praised by Ellsworth as the "originator of most of the new ideas planning of library building, resulted in modular, of loft-type, buildings with flexibility, allowing for adaptation of the building to constantly changing needs of collections, services, and staff. Earlier, flexibly was assumed with the removal of load-bearing walls from the interior of buildings, but today architects and librarians work togather to achieve ccmplete building module and attention (through the use of expert consultants) to the details of lighting, sound ventilation, and the Electro chemical aspects of building planning, A valuable body of literature on these subjects exists in the writings a Donald, Githens Thompson, Reece, Ellsworth, Met calf, and others, considerable attention to planning has been given by organisations such as the American Library Association (particularly its Buildings and equipment Section of the Library Administration Division and the Library Technology Programme supported by the Council on Library Resources, the Special Library Association, the Educational Facilities Laboratories (supported by Ford Foundation) the office of Education the U. S. Department of Health Education and Welfare, and various state local agencies Library Journal addresses itself to improved library facilities once in a year with its special December issue on "Architecture".

Flexibility continues to make greater demands on library planners today as the library function is defined to include recorded information in all its variants forms and media planning in several recent instances has resulted in libraries as "learning centers" utilizing much technologically advanced equipments. Examples of the centers can be found in Stephens College and Oral Roberts University-indeed, through the introduction of more advanced system of communication (improved microforms, audio, video, and computer tapes with computer perafaries, fascimile and data transmission capabilities, dial-access information system ; and the possible electro chemical combination of these), some writers have described the library of future not as buildingor a "place" at all but rather, as suggested by c walker stone (Library Tends, October, 1967), "AS A FAR = FLUNG net work composed of units of various sizes and types, each of which mayper form similaras well as different functions, but all of which will be linked together electro-mechanically."

nThis, library building planners have always concerned

themselves with function. In many notable instances they have erred when adapting the function plan of an earlier era to the needs of a library whose function is radically different. The moment-type library was origin ally connected with a temple or cathaderal and functioned well as such, but when this type of architecture was used in modern times to serve the urban library needs or open-access campus libraries, they were ill-thought, ill-planned or ill-served. All library buildings planning should start start with carefully detailed programming. In which the functional needs of the library are described, the proper type plan, or form, will follow. If the library building of the future is started from this base, it will be as great an accomplishments the library of Ephesus (A. D. 107) the bibliotheque Sainte Genevive (1843), o the success full John M olein library at Cornell University 1965 The public library building, in, the municipal library distinct from state and federal or national libraries, received its greatest impetus in the early 20th century from Carnegie Corporation. Not only did the carnegie corporation give money for the construction public library building but it also instructed that these buildings hold be community centersand issued in 1911, its NOTES ON THE ERECTION OF LIBRARARY BUILDING. Although the tremendous sociocultural impact and benefits of.the Carnegie Corporation's work cannot be denied.

It should be asserted that its NOTES were nearly leathel to continued imaginative planing in the design of library building for they tended to standardize library planning. Their's was not only the single great force of the time ; their design was emulated, of copied by others, Thus, the Carnegie Library of Syracause university, though much larger, is not unlike the earlier Carnegie Public Library of small communities through out the nation, and all bear close resemblance to the library at ephesus, their classical prototype, The NOTES of 1911 sought to overcome the classical plan by sustituting the "Carnegie rectangle" ? Which remained the standard of the library planning until the mid-1960's.

It was the post world war II period with its, sputinik, scientific and cultural advances publications and population explosion, computerisation, and advances in communication technology which demanded – with force – a freedom from the "carnegie - rectangle." A few notable breaks had been effected before the was thorough the works of Augus snead Mac Donaldand Alferd Morton Getheins. Mac-Donald, the originator of the modular concept, had been successfulness creating a module equally able to accomodate books or readers for library of congress Aannexe in the 1930s, several of the larger public libraries in Europe and America had sucessessfully functioning buildings at the same time, e.g, The Clevend Public Library (1925) and the Enoch Pratt Free Library at Baltimore (1933). It was the success of the Cleveland Public Library which set the trend for subject departmentalization in the major public library buildings. Since the war, the modular concept have been used used almost universally in public library buildings. Fine post war examples are the grosse point, Michigan Public Library (1953); the Seattle Public Library (1960); the Norfolk Public Library (1962); the addition to the Detrroit Public Library (1963); the Bufelo and Eric County Public Library (1964); the Knoxville branch, Carnegie library of Pitsberg (1965); the Edmonton, Alberta, public library (1967).

In the history of libraries, elementry and secondary school libraries are relatively recent having their development almost completely in the present century. Imaginative planning for school libraries consisted of one room, often poorly located with relation to other instructional and functional facilities of the school. The school library has followed the same evolution noted for public libraries. The one room library took the form of the right/left plan. Later, as newer instruction and communications technologies were developed, other rooms of the school building were given over to house their related facilities and services. They were sometimes adjacent to the library rooms, but more then not; in many instances, they were even administratively separated from the library function.

Recently, following an emphasis on the instructional function of library, plans have been effected in which first class library facilities are providedfor the newer schools. These libraries provide a full range of recorded materials and dinstructional media. They have been carefully planned with consltants' advice on electromechanical requirements and attention to lighting. Acoustics, airconditioning and all aspects of study comfort .

In a one-building school, the library has been located centrally in the main traffic area of the building, easily accessible to students, teachers, and administrators. Work space for library staff has been provided adjecent to the materials, which they service, yet removed from the student study areas. In the "campus" pinafore the newer secondary schools, the library is usually a separate, centerally heoteted building. Both elementry and secondary school today recognize the need for a variety of library seatings with special. Attention being given to individual study spaces, particularly carrels.

In an effort to establish more school libraries and improve existing ones, the American Library Association has declared," Every child needs a school library, and has issued its standards for school Libraries program (19 as a guide to school planners. This publication covers all aspects of school library services and to school planners. This publication covers all aspects of school library services and includes as an appendix. Policies and specifications for linrary quartes and equipment. The 1960 Standards has been replaced by standards for school Media programs (1969), which includes a chapterentitled Media cents centre Facilities". These publications were prepared by the American Association of School Libraries, a division of American, and the Department of Audio-Visual Instructions of the National Association of Education in cooperation wit the representatives of severall other library and educational association. School Library Programmes and quarter have improved nationally as a result of acceptance of these standards.)

A significant post world war II development has been the establishment of sperate undergraduate facilities on the large university campus. Two widely publicized examples are the Lamount

Library fat Harvard and the Undergraduate librarary at the University of Michigan. Amore recent example is the Henery meyer memorial library at stanford university. At Cornell and the University of California at Laos Angeles new research libraries. Have been builtand the former main library is now being used as an undergraduate libraries at cornell, extensive remodelling and renovation have resulted in a virtually new interior facility that combines the charm of the 1890 structure with all the comfortsand conviences of present day construction. The original structure of the building has actually been enhanced, yet its 1890 president Andrew D White library quarters have been restred, using to original tables and monet viena bentwood chairs, interior stone carvings, mantels, and fireplaces have been restored the entire building has been have had wood panelling instlled and lighting in proved the entire building has been airconditioned.

In recent years the college and university library buildings heave followed the success of the "liearning center" concept of the secondary schools. Notably, at the newly established campuses but also at some older campuses (e. g. stephen college), the learning center combines in one facility the traditional library lending and reference services with the newer communication technology through electro mechanical devices. Thus, as Oral Robert's University, the learning Resources Centerincludes television, studios, graphics studios. Dial-access information, systems (both audio and video), lecture halls with rear-view projection and TV monitors, classrooms with all modern teaching aids, and the full range of recorded mediacapabilities in the library portions of building.

Probably the heaviest use of the diel-audio systems that located at the hiostate university, where 40,000 calls per week were served through its dial are servediced through the dial-access information system. Here the system is seperated from the libraries physically from the libraries physically and administratively, he system is head quatered in Denny Hall, the liberal arts building, and information is carried by coaxil cable to points scattered about the campus;

doramatories in several locations, and the school of Nursing public utility lines carry the information to several fraternity houses situated near campus. The student union, the centeral library, commons (cafeteris) the music building and the. The information is stored on audio tapes which are activated through a special purpose computer by the dials at any of these remote location. The system were planned for audio use only, but has since been adapted to include some video stations. Another interseing approach is that installed at the okahoma christian college, where each of the 800 students enrolled at the college has a private Carrolin the Learning Center, which is capable of utilizing several types of teaching aids and an audio dial-access system. The cost of these elaborate installations is questioned by those who believe that high speed individual tape to tape duplication is more economical.

In future, more libraries will take on the role of "instructional" or learning centers as dial-access systems and and computer assisted instructions system are added to the more traditional functions of printed media. The building problem of such centers are simply those of every greater-flexibility. To the need for providing flexibility in air conditioning lighting and partitioning, must be added the capability of carrying audio-visual signals throughout the building, and indeed, out side the building and the other parts of the college and university campus. Such a building is but the first step towards an electromechanical communications network of service on a local, regional, national and international basis. Thus , the library of the future day truly may not a "place" but a far-flung system of interconnected facilities and stations.

Libraries organised to serve particular clientele are refered to as special Libraries. Typically, they are found in the centeral of major plants of industrial and commercial firms banks, hospitals, research organisations and government agencies, but the branch or departmental libraries of the universities are not unlike them in their organisation, services, and physical arrangement. The nature of collection of then presents special housing problems. Special shelving or storage equipment installed to house substantial collection of maps, reports literature, blueprints, photographs and newspaper clippings are not uncommon of stapedial concern to some is the provsion for a vault or separate storage room to house substantial collections of classified documents. Typical layouts for special library are those of the Engineering staff Library of the Ford Motors Company and the library of the Mead Corpn. Because the tendency is to decenterlize special library services, large special libraries are seldom found. Generally, twenty to fifty readers seats are sufficient and the total space allotted to the library is 2,000 to 10,000 squaire feet. Special libraries have set the pace for documentation and advanced methods for information handeling and it is not unusual and it is not usual to find data-processing centers near, adjecent to, or integrated with the special library. The Special Library Association has published its" objectives and standards for special libraries" (special Libraries, December, 1964), which includes an "Appendix : standard specification, giving the physical space and equipment standards for a special library, SPECIAL LIBRARY, the association's journal carries features, articleson library plans, layout, equipment, and organisation.

The American Library Association headquarters' library and the Library Technology Programme maintain collection of prints, slides, architectural drawings of buildings and equipment, the building programme statements, all of which are available to librarians through out the world through interlibrarry loan. In recent years, library schools have sponsered seminars and workshops on building ;planning and the building equipment section of the library administration division of the American Library Association sponsors preconferences are published regularly. These activities of the library schools and professional organisation carry forward the interests of library building planners today.

ARCHITECTURE, LIBRARY BUILDING

The architectural design, nature, and quality of contemporary academic library buildings in the United States, Great Britain, and, to a lesser extent, in western Europe results from a number of factors: historical precedents, customs, and fashions; the size of library collections; the size of the reading population involved; the nature of the library's purpose, function, and use; the state of building technology; the state of communication technology; environmental factors, including campus plan, site, climate, and degree of air pollution; the librarian--his ability and freedom; external controls exercised by attitudes, and ability and freedom; external controls exercised by governmental agencies or private donors; and, last, the status of the library as a symbol of the measure of man's respect for the power of knowledge and learning.

Each of these are discussed primarily from the point of view of academic libraries in the United States and Great Britain. A few examples from northern Europe will be cited.

Historical Precedents, Customs, and Fashions

Before World War II, in the United States on the academic campus, one could usually identify the library building by its location and its monumental character, but there was no specific library style or design that was an inevitable expression of the functions performed within the buildings. To some extent the same could be said of the municipal library buildings in the United States, except that the Carnegie buildings tended to shape the library functions to fit the interior plan of the buildings. Academic library buildings were created in whatever classical style was in favor at the time, such as Greek and Roman, Gothic, Romanesque, Italian Hillside, Southwestern Indian Pueblo, or some other recognizable style. Typical examples would be the Northwestern University and Temple University central library buildings; the Low Library at Columbia University and the central library of the University of North Carolina; the central libraries of the Universities of Missouri, Illinois, New Mexico, and Colorado. The old library at Grinnell College was a typical Carnegie college library building, of which there were many other examples in the country. Most of these buildings copied the predominant architectural style of their campus—the Universities of Chicago, Duke, and Colorado, for example—but occasionally an architect introduced a new kind of style. However, this was always one that was historically familiar. The Gothic Cathedral and the Roman and Greek Temple had been the most commonly known types used in the United States, Great Britain, and Europe. The University of New Mexico is probably the best example of the use of a local indigenous architectural style—the Indian Pueblo. Among the newer buildings, the Indiana University library's use of native limestone is another example of the use of indigenous materials.

But at the end of World War II, because of new thinking about all the above factors, especially in building and communication technology and in architectural design, new architectural styles for libraries began to evolve. The modular method of planning could have been used in any of the traditional styles [as, indeed, was done in the Princeton library, which was a kind of Gothic structure liberally diluted by Main Street First Presbyterian Church architecture— a most appropriate style for the setting, but it was obvious that it would be most efficiently used in a square or rectangular-shaped building as was done at the University of Iowa, North Dakota State College, and Hardin-Simmons. These boxes used a conventional skin as at Iowa or the University of California at Los Angeles Research Library, San Fernando Valley, andChico or glass walls as at Michigan State University and the University of Chicago Law Library. The Washington University library in St. Louis, which is in reality a square box was perhaps the first large academic library to present an exterior architecture that obviously evolved from the needs of the internal functioning of the building. It used recognizable materials, shapes, proportions, and lines, but it bore no surface resemblance to the nearby Gothic Chapel or the adjacent academic buildings, which were modified Georgian in style. Nor did this library look like any other modular libraries on other campuses. Since that time many other architects have developed designs that are unique to each building. A few examples of such academic libraries are found in the following institutions: Brown, Hofstra, Chabot, Grinnell College, Earlham, The University of Baltimore, Oral Roberts, Boston University, The University of Massachusetts, Arizona State University, the Knoxville branch of the Carnegie library in Pittsburgh, and The Nogales, Arizona Public Library. The Gate School in California and the Foothills Junior College library in California are examples of school and junior college libraries. Many branch libraries in large city systems are outstanding in their uniqueness. In Europe the Chalmers Technological Institute in Sweden, Bonn University, the Caen University library in France, the Saarbrucken, and the Stuttgart Technischen Hochschule in Germany are outstanding.

In fact, the trend toward originality to design these library buildings is so strong today that any new library building that bears a surface resemblance to an existing one causes the raising of professional eyebrows.

The opening of many new institutions has given architects an opportunity to design entire campuses all at once, in a more or less unified style. The new regional "Robbins" Universities in England, such as Essex or Lancaster, tend to be of this nature, but in Sussex each building is different from others on the campus. The Eugenia Atwood Library at the new Beaver College Campus near Philadelphia is an example of a unified campus structure in the United States. Other examples are Stephens College, the Foothills Junior College in California, and the new College of Santa Fe inNeV Mexico. In Europe institutions do not usually follow the unified architectural concept, although the new campus of Oslo University does to some extent. New libraries different in character from other buildings on campus are to be found in such places as Glasgow, Edinburgh, Sussex, Giessan, Bonn, Stuttgart, and Chalmers, to name only a few. The new library of the Crackow School of Mines in

Poland, one of the first, if not the first, modular library in Europe, has its own unique design.

Architectural fads and fashions are naturally not always identifiable as such until a period of time has elapsed, but some contemporary ones are easy to detect.

1. "The library in the round" as a phrase has great appeal to academic administrators who crave change for its own sake and to architects who are bored with the traditional square or rectangular-shaped library. Experience shows that the circle is not a good shape for a library because it results in a very inflexible interior, causes clumsy furniture layouts, creates traffic patterns that are confusing to the public, and is wasteful of space; in spite of these facts, however, the idea has much appeal. There is one small round library that is very successful — a branch of the Newcastle-upon-the Tyne Public Library, designed by Harry Brown. Its success arises from its size as well as the architect's genius.
2. The atrium, an open space in the middle of a building, once necessary to provide light and ventilation for readers but no longer necessary for these reasons, has been and continues to be a real barrier to an efficiently arranged building, especially a large university library building.

Early versions of plans for the new library at New York University by Philip Johnson had a large atrium extending from the main floor to the roof. This resulted in a horseshoe-shaped interior with quite narrow side areas. This atrium obviously was put there for design purposes only; it had no relationship to function and would have interfered seriously with the functioning of the library. On the other hand, a small atrium properly located in a relatively small building such as those found in the Mount St. Scholastica Library in Atchison, Kansas the Stephens College library in Columbia, Missouri, or the Washington University library in St. Louis, does very little harm to function and is a nice flourish of a traditional nature. An atrium inserted above the main floor level of the library, such as in the Tutt Library at Colorado College, causes only a small inconvenience to readers. An example of a serious misuse of an atrium can be found in the La Junta High School building in Colorado, where the entirefront of the library, located on the second floor, constitutes the front wall of a two-story atrium which in turn is the front entrance lobby of the building. The noise caused by hundreds of students milling around between classes is so loud there that the library is unusable at these times.

A variant of the atrium, used at Georgia Institute of Technology, Grinnell, and Rice, in which the floor levels are high enough to accommodate a two-tier stack as a spine running from one end of the building to the other, can be charming in the conventional sense, but it tends to result in an inflexible building and one that is difficult to remodel, as Rice University has discovered in recent years.

Another variant, found in law libraries in which John Hervey, a member of the staff of the American Bar Association, has been involved, has a mezzanine opening off the main reading room. Current periodicals are usually kept on the mezzanine. Just why readers of current periodicals must first climb a flight of steps to get at their material is not entirely clear.

3. The tower, generally thought to be a thoroughly unsatisfactory shape for a library after the experience of Texas, Rochester, and the University of Pittsburgh, has appeared again in recent years with all the old disadvantages but under circumstances which might justify it, such as a campus like New York University where land for a horizontal library simply does not exist. This form has also been advocated by the chairman of the Building Committee of the Board of Trustees of the California State College system as a substitute for the large block-shaped li-brary buildings that are necessary to contain the work of these very large campuses, even when space is not at a premium.

4. The glass box, fashionable at the end of World War II, seemed to express a need to "bring the outdoors in," although no one is quite sure what you do withthe outdoors in a library, particularly when the outdoors is not conducive to reading or when it is unsightly or uninteresting. Colored, heat-resistant glass, draperies, Venetian blinds, and exterior baffles are some of the devices that architects have been forced to use to reduce the heat and glare in the glass wall libraries; and special heat injectors located at the base of the exterior glass walls have been necessary to warm readers who would like to sit near the walls. An example of this is found in the Grinnell College library.
5. Rigid use of symmetry in locating the fixed elements in a building, particularly when the entrance is in the middle of a fagade, creates difficulties in developing an efficient main floor arrangement of a library because the divisions that must go on the main floor, i.e., reference, circulation, technical processing, current periodicals, administrative offices, and so forth, are not all the same size and do not therefore necessarily match the spaces left for them. This is particularly handicapping in a small building (see the Grinnell College library).
6. Architectural cliches and flourishes, such as long flights of exterior steps at Sussex in England the grand interior stairway at Colorado State University, the excessive use of new materials such as colored panels or precast brushed cement panels, the use of blond furniture in the 1950s as in the University of Houston Library, or the fondness of architects for spotlights for interior lighting (see the Yale University Art Library), rapidly became dated and soon became a frightful bore.

Size of Collections to be Housed

Although architects have, in modern times at least, always

had to design libraries that could be enlarged to take care of growing book collections, the problem of size did not create a design problem until in recent years when the rate of growth accelerated as a result of the so-called knowledge explosion. The size of the book storage problem was such that it could be handled in one of the classical architectural styles or forms without destroying the scale or proportion of the form. The New York Public Library, Widener Library at Harvard, and Sterling Library at Yale housed large collections, but expansion occurred outside of the central library buildings and not by continuous adding to these buildings, which would have been impossible. The problem of how to give architectural character to a library building that requires additions every decade or so is a challenging one to architects. Likewise, the problem is acute in an institution when it knows that it is to be a college today or a university tomorrow (for example, Central MichiganState University or the Baptist College of Charleston in South Carolina), when an institution takes on a new dimension (such as Wells College facing the prospect of adding to a men's college in the future, adjacent to the present campus) that requires a quite different kind of size of book collection, or when a state agency imposes policies on existing institutions that cause a radical shift in their enrollment patterns (see the 1967 Recommendations of the Colorado Commission on Higher Education and the potential shifts in the California University system's enrollments if changes in the financing patterns, as proposed by Governor Reagan, should be adopted). In these cases the question of architectural style and design for a library becomes acute and virtually rules out the possibility of using a fixed-function type of building. The basic assumption behind a fixed-function library was that the ratios between the space needs of books and readers were predictable and unchanging. The modular libraries permit continuous interchange in use of space without major reconstruction. They can also be enlarged without destroying unity of service or architectural design.

New techniques for storing printed matter electronically or

in microforms affect not only the quantity of space needed but also the characteristics of this space. For example, the various types of storage systems—the drawer systems by Ames and Hamilton—require special floor load requirements and do not permit the use of a high-rise stack system; the movable stack range systems with one aisle serving a block of ranges, such as used by Compactus, require floors capable of carrying very heavy loads and space in the floors for cables and wheels; the use of narrow stack aisles for storage requires extra strong floors. All types require special lighting and sometimes special ventilation.

New electronically controlled storage systems, such as Randtriever retrieval systems proposed in 1967 by the Sperry Rand Corporation, have not been in actual use; thus it is impossible to draw conclusions as to usefulness, cost, and effect on architecture. But if these systems do prove to be satisfactory, they undoubtedly will require specially designed storage space.

The introduction of new containers for knowledge (microforms, computer tapes, phonograph records and tapes, and TV tapes) do not impose unusual storage problems, but their use does require special facilities. These new forms could affect the number of books in original form that a library would need to store.

Size of Reader Population to be Served

The size of the reader population to be served in educational institutions has changed radically in the last 150 years. The typical arts college, for example, in the nineteenth century was open only a few hours per week and contained only a few seats for readers. In the 1960s a high-quality institution finds it necessary to provide seats for from 35 to 65% of their student bodies. Even the California State College system assumes that seats for 25% are essential. These changes reflect not only the maturing of new disciplines (the sciences, the social sciences, and the new professional schools), but also the quantity of knowledge there is tobe learned and the methods of teaching that require students to dig out their own source material from the world of print instead of taking their information solely from class lectures and textbooks. Perhaps they are also a reflection of the needs of new kinds of students in a system of mass, impersonal education, although this is a subjective judgment.

Faculties, too, require special study space in the library to an extent that is radically different from what it was in the past. Young married men with large families, living in apartments and small houses, cannot study at home; nor can they afford their own private research collections. They must now rely on the library for their source material. The "publish or perish" slogan, even when it is not used literally, does mean that the university's professor is expected to do research. And, in the larger and better private colleges, the professor-scholar is still held up as the ideal, even though in the smaller colleges a man may not be required to do much research. There are few institutions in which the faculty can get by with teaching alone.

University libraries located in or near cities where research laboratories exist (and all but a few are so located) find heavy use of their scientific collections by scholars not connected with the university. Ten percent of the total use consisting of use of this nature is not uncommon, and in institutions like Rochester and MIT, it might go considerably higher. This use frequently involves photocopying machinery.

Two other new kinds of use of college and university libraries have emerged in the 1960s: (1) extensive use by college-educated citizens who find public libraries' collection inadequate, except in the larger cities; and (2) use by high school students who now find high school libraries of little value to them at a time when extensive improvements in teaching make strong library collections imperative. In 1963 there were not six public high school libraries with as many as 20,000 books in them in the United States.

Nature of the Library's Purpose, Function, and Use

Prior to the use of artificial light, heat, and ventilation, the exterior architecture of the library building was determined by its purpose and use to a far greater extent than has been true since the adoption of these mechanical operations, especially the building's fenestration. For example, the exterior design of the Beineke Rare Book Library at Yale gives no clue as to the type of library within, nor could one judge from the exterior of Johns Hopkins' new central library that it might not be a storage library. On the other hand, the Midwest Inter-Center [now called the Center for Research Libraries] exterior suggests that it is indeed a storage library.

On the inside of the newer buildings, however, the architecture of the contemporary libraries *is* determined largely by the purpose and use of the building, and the resulting patterns are fairly obvious. Rare book libraries (such as Houghton at Harvard, Beineke at Yale, or Lilley at Indiana) are designed to provide optimum condition of storage and preservation for rare books. Reader facilities are usually elegant in nature and are so located that they can be carefully supervised. They occupy only a small part of the building. Specially designed rooms to house special collections, sometimes recreated from the donor's home, are frequently provided. Rather sumptuous quarters for mature scholars are not uncommon.

Most college libraries and all but the largest universities provide direct access to the bookstack by readers, and this calls for an interior architectural design that will fuse the book and reader spaces in such a manner as to encourage direct use. This has been done in such a wide variety of ways that generalizations are not only impossible but unnecessary. Most of the newer university libraries in Great Britain use the open-access principle (Lancaster, Sussex, and Exeter, to mention only a few), but few of the continental libraries have done so. In Europe one frequently finds a movable-belt system of delivery from the bookstacks to the main desk, but lack of staff slows down delivery time to such an extent that the machinery efficiency is wasted. In fact, in some places, it is not even used.

The modular method of planning in the new buildings is

almost universally used, even when the bookstacks are grouped in a solid block on each floor; thusthe possibility of an interchange of use for any given floor area is kept open. This definitely does affect the architectural design.

The modular library building is in direct contrast to the fixed-function building which was in common use until World War II. In the latter, space for books was provided in a specific part of a building in a multitier bookstack, each with thin floors and ceiling heights of approximately 7 feet, 2 inches. Reading rooms were designed as architectural entities, the heights of which were sometimes not correlated with stack levels, and in all cases were two or more levels in height. The two-on-one ratio was used throughout by only two university libraries prior to World War II—Colorado and Virginia. In the fixed-function buildings, there was little possibility of interchange of use, and unless the ratios between books and readers fitted the changing need of the institution, the building rapidly became obsolete. Grand staircases and elegant lobbies, long flights of exterior steps, and lavish use of materials characterized these buildings. Typical examples are Sterling at Yale, Widener at Harvard, Low at Columbia, and the central library of the University of Michigan at Ann Arbor. The University of Southern California and Temple would be other examples.

In the modular building all spaces, except for the fixed elements, such as toilets, stairwells, lobbies, and so forth, are capable of housing all typical library functions. The structure is supported by columns, regularly spaced. Subdivisions are created by nonbearing walls, bookstacks, and free-standing furniture. Horizontal ducts are carried between the floor structure and a suspended ceiling which contains the light fixtures. There are, of course, many kinds of lighting systems. Ceiling heights vary from 8 to 9 feet, or even 10 feet, but 8 feet, 6 inches is frequently used. Floor-to-floor dimensions usually require an extra *lVz* to 2 feet for ducts, wiring, and so forth. Artificial air and lighting can be brought to any part of the building.

In a fixed-function building the plan of organization determines, or should at least do so, the architectural scheme of the building. Before 1940 most all college and university libraries followed a single type of organization. A combination of general reference and reading room, a closed-access bookstack, a separate reserved book room, and special rooms for periodicals and newspapers, rare books, and technical processing was universally used. Seminar rooms are frequently located on the top floors of the buildings.

Two universities, Colorado and Nebraska, just before World War II, developed full-subject divisional reading room plans in fixed-function buildings. The size of the reading rooms was determined in advance and space ratios between readers and material was fixed. There was a formal division of labor among the various parts of the building.

Since World War II modular-type buildings have been used with both the old and new subject divisional type of organization and with variants. Some libraries have switched from one kind of an organization to another (the University of Iowa, for example).

Thus it is fair to say that in a modular building the influence of purpose and use is not a determining factor in fixing the architectural style and design as it was in the older fixed-function types of buildings.

The State of Building Technology

The use of steel framing and flat slab construction and nonbearing interior and exterior walls plus the ability to introduce artificial air and light at any place in the building have created an architectural problem of some magnitude. It can be stated as follows: Because of the rapid growth in book collections and in patterns of use, a good college or university library must have maximum adaptability qualities within its walls and must be capable of being expanded economically and functionally. State planning agencies usually insist on low-cost structures, that at the time of occupancy will operate 10 years before being expanded for another decade's use. The modular method of planning meets all the requirements, especially if it is developed in the shape of a box, square, or rectangle. But such a structure is not thought to be interesting according to traditional architectural concepts and does not give the architect a chance to design a building with a high-quality living environment as conceived in conventional terms. Thus the prima donna architects and those with conservative points of view have either resisted the modular type, have molded it into uneconomical shapes, or have infiltrated it with traditional architectural flourishes (atriums, for example), forgetting by so doing that the flourishes were merely the necessities of a more primitive building technology.

The Washington University in St. Louis is generally considered to be the first successful attempt where an architect used the modular method with architectural imagination, consistent with the new building technology. In the mean time there were dozens of "unimaginative" modular buildings that were successfully meeting the needs of their campuses [Iowa, Oregon (see Figure 20), Georgia, San Fernando Valley, for example] even though they lacked beauty in the traditional sense. This cannot be said of the nonmodular buildings built during the same period of time, especially when the problem of a building addition had to be faced (see Rice, Colorado, Nebraska, and MIT, for example).

The use of carpeting, new materials, colors, and interesting as well as comfortable furniture has revolutionized the moods of library buildings. (See the Cazenovia College Library as a fine example.) This use can be measured by the volume of circulation use and by the longer periods of time students study in the new buildings.

The most controversial question (and, in fact, the only one of any importance) evolving from the new building technology is a question of illumination—amount, intensity, and quality. Light fixture manufacturers and illuminating engineers tend to assume the more light one provides the better it is for the reader. Metcalf (see his book *Planning Academic and Research Library Buildings*, Chapter 9) and others maintain that relatively low-light levels under 50 foot candles are satisfactory for reading, if the quality of the light is high. There is a difference of opinion (See Mason's article "Lighting and Ventilation" in the *Library Journal*, January 15, 1967, p. 201-205) about how one determines good quality in lighting. At the time of writing, the issues have not been settled in such a way that there can be an objective, scientific way of defining quality of lighting.

On the question of ventilation, there seems to be an agreement that most artificially ventilated buildings are too hot and do not provide enough turnover of air to provide fresh air. Yet the problem may be one of economics rather than the state of the art of ventilation. Too frequently the client does not provide supervising engineering services capable of operating the new machinery. Sometimes the problem is simply one of keeping the thermostat too high to meet the needs of librarians whose habits are sedentary.

The large number of readers who are confined to the use of a wheelchair owing to World War II, the Korean War, and the Vietnam War has focused attention on the library entrance problem with their customary long flight of exterior steps. Nevertheless, most architects still fail to provide a ramp or other means of easy access for chair-ridden readers. Federal and some state laws now require ramps.

The State of Communication Technology

Printing from movable type formed the almost exclusive basis for nonoral communication until the 1930s when microfilm came into common use. The motion picture, although older than microfilm, had little effect until documentaries came into use in the 1940s and until closed-circuit television became a reality in the 1960s. All three media used the printed word exclusively. The computer, as a means of communication, is still in its early stages and is today pretty much confined to transmitting mathematical symbols and data. The computer cannot yet be used for transmitting, economically at least, the kind of dialogue that takes place when one reads, for instance, Kants' *Critique of Pure Reason.* Only a fool, however, would today place any limits on the future possibilities and application of computer communication.

The way in which each new media affects the architecture of library buildings can be summarized, fairly conservatively, in the following manner

MICROFORMS

The use of microforms will increase as ways are found of financing group filming projects for manuscript collections and other bodies of print that are not more economically accessible via the printing press. The medium could be used for original publishing of manuscripts for which there is a low and sporadic demand, in the manner doctoral dissertions are now published by the Educational Division of the Xerox Corporation. On the other hand, because of the large number of new libraries being created, it can be expected that reprint editions of the classics in all fields will appear at a cost considerably lower than microfilming can offer.

Microforms coordinated with computerized indexing and printout machines are already appearing on the market. Copyright laws may be a restricting factor—but not if the processor takes the trouble to charge royalties and to pay the controller of the copyright.

Large libraries that need to acquire source material will thus be acquiring microforms of titles not now owned. This will save some square footage in the book-stacks but will require more space for mechanical reading machines, so the gain is something in the order of 60 to 80%, not 100%. College libraries, too, will acquire some material in microforms in addition to newspaper and journal files, which all will buy, but not so much as will universities, because their programs dp not require large amounts of source material.

Very high-reduction microcopying projects, such as Verac.

are held back by the lack of satisfactory photo-enlarging machines and by the lack of organizations that can finance the costs involved in organizing film projects and preparing the films for sale. The overhead cost in selling prints from a large vault of microform negatives is high. If the operation could be automated, these costs might be lowered to the point that the use of microforms could become more attractive.

AUDIOVISUAL AIDS

Motion picture films and tapes and computer tapes—8, 16, and 35 mm—will need to be used by individuals in libraries, but this use can be accomplished by a closed-circuit television or portable viewers in the library, while the originals are kept in a laboratory some place else on campus. The connecting link (coaxial cables and telephone wires) between the reader seated at a portable television receiver with earphones and the world of films and tapes is a matter of economics, not engineering.

COMPUTERS

Libraries look forward to national, regional, and local data banks for all kinds of statistical data now available, if at all, in printed books.

Librarians can assume that eventually all bibliographic records will be put onto computers so that literature searching and bibliographic compilation work will bedone, not by raw searching through printed books and indexes, but by consulting their computer console. The cost of this service is not known today, but it is likely to be high—so high, in fact, that it will be beyond the reach of individuals without special financial support.

Librarians should not assume that the computer will relieve them of the necessity of maintaining reference staffs and services. On the contrary these operations will increase in sophistication and depth. There will be the added need of coordinating access between information available on the computer and in printed books.

Specialized knowledge of the terminology and computer thesauruses, catalogs, and bibliographies will be even more necessary than it is now in the usual reference library. Librarians cannot assume that the availability of data on the computer will eliminate the need for buying the books from which the data were taken. Computer access may not alone be good enough to meet the needs of researchers. Some actual scanning of the printed page itself may be necessary. The element of serendipity is not present in the computer. The kinds of networks of computerized bibliographic services and data exchanges now being studied by governments and organizations like *Educom* will be a great asset to librarians as well as researchers in their laboratories. Long-distance transmission of images of pages of print, now subject to experimentation, can be expected to be a superior substitute for inter-library lending as now practiced; but because of cost and technical limitations, it is not likely to become a leveler of library services. [See the experiment by the University of Nevada and the University of California (Davis Campus) in using the facsimile service as a substitute for interlibrary lending practices.] Transmission systems based on a bank of microforms, with computerized bibliographic controls, offer considerable promise when technical and financial limitations are removed.

Therefore the computer may save a small amount of space in libraries in terms of books that no longer need to be bought, but they will increase the amount of space needed for computer consoles, printout enlargers, and other hardware. They will also increase the need for larger reference staffs. They will require soundproof rooms, and since they will be used in the technical processing and the clerical operations at the charging desks and other places, one can anticipate higher cost library buildings as soon as computers are used.

Environmental Factors: Site, Climate, Air Pollution, and the like

The site is one of the major factors determining the architectural character of the library building. If surrounding buildings possess a strong architectural expression but do not harmonize with the expression the architect has in mind for the library, he may have trouble convincing the client whose knowledge of such matters is usually fairly unsophisticated. The height of the building may be limited by the roof lines of the surrounding buildings. Unless the site permits sufficient space for future expansion that fits the needs of the campus plan, it may not be suitable at all. In theory a library building should be sunk into the ground so that the mainentrance divides the building in two vertically. Unfavorable excavation and water level conditions may make this impossible or too expensive. For economy of operation, a library building should have only one entrance and exit point. This is difficult if the building is in the middle of the center of a campus. It is easy if the building is along the edge of the center. The contours of the site (a steep hillside, for example, at Cincinnati and Johns Hopkins dictated a top-floor entrance) may determine the entire architectural expression.

Temperature ranges, amount of precipitation, wind conditions, and amount of sunshine affect not only the appropriateness of various architectural types, but also such fundamental matters as fenestration, air conditioning, insulation, nature of the entrance vestibule and lobby, floor coverings, and so forth. The amount of air pollution will determine whether or not an electronic filter system is necessary.

The Architect: His Style, Wishes, Competence, and the like

Of all the factors involved, the architect is probably the most important because he is usually in a position to make the final decisions on all the other factors. Since architecture is an art, it is inevitable that there be a wide range of talent, imagination, and practicality among architects. Anyone who has studied the library as a. building type, or who has visited critically the hundreds of new buildings erected in the United States since World War II, is forced to the conclusion that they run the gamut between success and failure in terms of the criteria of beauty, utility, and economy--

but seldom does an architect operate in a vacuum. A building may be a failure not because of the architect, but because the client failed to program the building's nature, capacities, and future uses properly; or the client may have imposed aesthetic or budgetary limitations that create difficulties for the architect. Thus in judging a particular building, one must know all the factors that determine its nature.

The following characteristics seem be necessary in an architect who consistently designs good library buildings:

1. An attitude of willingness to think of a library building not as an abstract work of art but as a place where certain important human activities are to be performed. The degree to which the building permits these activities to be performed in a manner that is natural, pleasant, comfortable, and joyful to people will determine the success of the building and therefore its beauty.
2. An attitude of scholarliness which will lead the architect to discover what the client expects the building to do. If he finds that the client does not know how to decide the building's function, he, the architect, will have to make certain that one way or another a good program is developed.
3. Special ability is required to translate a program into a structure that is beautiful, functional, and economical. Architects differ in the extent to which they possess this talent. They are judged by their results. Beauty as a relative function can be rated by the criteria stated in the literature (see Metcalf, *Planning Academic and Research Library Buildings*, and Ellsworth, *Planning College and University Library Buildings*, 1963); costs can be gathered and used as a basis for comparisons.

The use of a building consultant to help with the development of a program and with the evaluation of the architect's plans has come to be standard procedure. The consultant's work gives the architect and the client the assurance that a satisfactory and complete program is prepared. The building institutes sponsored by the American Library Association can provide a sense of group evaluation of plans, but lack of knowledge of the local site problems can lead to misdirected criticisms. For example, the "evaluation by correspondence" of the plans for the Southern Colorado College in Pueblo by experts who should have known better failed to take into consideration that there are times when departures from complete practicability can be justified by other factors. Fortunately the architects, Caudill and Rogers, were wise enough to ignore that kind of advice. The results justified their wisdom.

4. Humility in sufficient quantity to enable an architect to profit by criticism. It is this lack of humility that has led to the repetition of errors in planning that make so many libraries less satisfactory than they should be. The law library at the University of Chicago, the Grinnell library, the Colorado State University library, and the Air Force Academy library are four outstanding examples of a lack of humility in architects. Since World War II, a rather peculiar situation has developed in the United States that has been a handicap to many able architects. Although this is a personal judgment of the author, the matter may be stated in the following way: Americans seem to have an inferiority complex about their feeling for architectural beauty. They express their uneasiness by clinging to the symbols of success. Sometimes this means architects with a foreign background and sometimes architects who for reasons that are not based on their work achieve a position of glamour. These men establish and set the tone that lesser architects, whose work may be far superior, must follow if they are to receive commissions. This situation has definitely been a handicap in the development of library buildings that might be honest and strong expressions of their utility. The problem isinherent in the basic architectural dilemma, which is that while a building may be a pure art form, it must be used by people. and this use may require

architectural expressions that do not coincide with traditional concepts of beauty.

External Controls, Good and Bad, Have Determined the Architectural Quality of Many Buildings

The low standards imposed by some state boards and departments of architecture have made planning difficult in such states as California and Tennessee, for example. Donors' conditions are legion. Misguided advice by the client—presidents, librarians, faculty library committees, and even consultants—have not always been overcome by their architects. Few examples of distinguished architecture have come out of states where state boards of architecture (California, New York, and Wisconsin, for example) have been given responsibility for designing library buildings. The reason is probably that first-rate architects do not want to work for state boards or to submit to the conditions imposed by governments. The Federal government, fortunately, has in its Federal support programs left the planning of specific buildings to the clients.

The Library as a Symbol of Man's Evaluation of Knowledge and Learning

Although the judgment is subjective, a case can be made for the idea that the architectural expression and character of the library reflects the degree of reverence and respect the public has for knowledge and learning. Some of the respect of knowledge and learning rubs off on the containers or carriers of that knowledge —the book and the house of books. Thus the Carnegie Public Library, around the turn of the century, was interpreted as the peoples' university: thus the axiom that the library building should be monumental because it is the heart of the university. Almost always the library is given a touch of elegance which is denied the classroom building, college dormitory, or science building. It is for the same reason that these qualities are sometimes given to the art studio, where the same kind of respect is placed.

But in recent years the prestige of scientific knowledge and the decline in prestige in the humanities and the knowledge derived from the humanities and the social sciences (unless they are behavioral) is beginning to be reflected in the architectural treatment of science buildings on the campus. No longer are they mere workshops. They possess *mana,* and they therefore deserve the architectural elegance [see the new biophysics buildings at Yale and the NCAR buildings in Boulder, Colorado (Figure 22)] that was once reserved for the central library, which is, in fact, primarily the house for the literature of the humanities and the social sciences on the university campuses.

This shift in symbolism is reflected in the fact that although many of the new libraries on the campuses are still monumental, this is usually not allowed to crowd out the factor of utility. Most of the new buildings are modular, and they are very functional. Some of the best examples are the new research library at UCLA, Cornell, Washington University, Earlham College, Indiana University, Hofstra University, Oregon, Colorado College, Cazenovia College, Beloit College, Beaver College, Southern Methodist University Science Library, Mt. St. Scholastica in Atchinson, and Austin Peay State College.

Some Special Problems

The peculiar dilemma faced by architects and librarians in planning new academic libraries is the uncertainty about how much access and what kind of access to provide for electronic-learning hardware. Providing outlets through the floor for jacks and plugs is unsightly. Providing conduits in permanent walls is one solution. Providing access through the ceilings (between the structure and the suspended ceiling) is easy in a modular library because the wiring can be brought down through the columns and across the reading room carrells, with portable hardware plugged into jacks and outlets in the carrells.

The per-square-foot costs of a modern academic library

building are high, primarily because of air-conditioning costs and because of the highly sophisticated provisions that must be made for electronic-learning hardware. It is clear that there are now many media for learning, and the individual can expect the library to provide the necessary conditions for all their use.

The requirements is terms of fiances are estimated as 6-12% of the total budget outlay of the parent institution or to decide any on head and to calculate other heads on proportionate percentage. For regular and recurring budget to the allocation is based upon internal comparative percentage of different heads and for non recurring expenditures the estimates are prepared on the basis of quantitative and qualitative requirements.

7.1 U.G.C. GRANTS BUDGETING

Since 1961 Central Government grants are being allocated to the universities in India on play basis through University Grants Commission India. The Grants paid for library are detailed with a few directives. Those are the total outlay is usually for a period of Five years and is to be phased in the assigned period, 20% of the book budget grant can be spent on staff for the utilisation of the graht purchase of reading material and its processing. 5% of the U.G.C. Grant for the library can be spent on stacking material for the reading material purchased. Thus, 75% U.G.C. Grants left over the purchase of reading material. Again this allocation is to be divided o 50:50 basis, thus amounts to 37.5% for purchase of textbooks for under-graduates and post-graduates and 37.5% is spent on research treatises and back volumes of periodicals (In no case subscription for current periodicals is to be paid out of U.G.C. Grant).

But, unfortunately the state universities are so tight as far as financial resources are concerned that they violate the conditions laid down by U.G.C. For U.G.C. Grants internal budgeting and their allocation for subject wise is the responsibility of the individual university library with the help of the library committee members representing the teaching and research departments.

7.2 Some Issues for consideration

1. How to prepare budget for a library?
2. How to utilize budgeting techniques for library as used by commercial and industrial organisation?
3. How to adjust new techniques to evaluate library programmes regular as well as development?

Included here, in this lesson, is loud thinking regarding University library buildings as a vital input for the efficiency of library functioning. The points discussed are :

1. Team for Planning-Architect to cooperative venture
2. Planning Principles
3. Architectural Styles
4. Location and internal shape plans
5. Space allocation for different purposes

Helpfull Readings

1. DEWELT (Robert E): 'Control Key to making financial strategies work', Management Review, March, 1977, p. 20.

2. IRVINE (V. Bruce) "Budgeting; Functional Analysis and Behavioural Implications". In cost of and Management V44, no2; March/ April, 1970 pp6-16.

3. TLEY (D.T): "Budget Use and Management Performance". Journal of Accounting Research. V16; 1978. pp 122-149.

4. DECOSTER (Don T.) "Management Accounting; A Decision Emphasis" and ELDON (L.

Scdhafer) New York, John Willey, 1982. pp. 489-514.

5. ARGYRIS (Chris): Human problems with budgets. Harvard Business Review Jan-Feb, 1950. p, 150.

Includes a note on University Library Building since U.G.C's assistance. Refers to Indian Standards and suggests their updating.

A. LIBRARY BUILDING : PROGRAMMING AND PLANNING

1. Era of Architects

"Inadequate attention was given to proper programming with the result that architects did to much of the planning on their own responsibility. In almost all articles written prior to 1931, it is complained that librarian has altogether been ignored in the building planning programme. Richard offer reported, "that three of four libraries in England had been planed without a librarian". The news item of 18802 term, "the architect as the natural enemy of the liberation."

2. To Librarians :

The vital role of the librarian in planning has been emphasized by Mauran as early as 1901, "the problem presented to an architect by a library board is always essentially a new one. Certain fundamental rules may obtain through their universal applicability, but every step in the working out of a successful plan must be influenced by the particular conditions referred to, thus the cooperation of the librarian is of inestimable value to the architects." A shift in trend, after continued hue and cry by the librarians, has been reported by Raney. "For the two building I had prepared building plans and had obtained faculty and administrative approval before an architect was hired. All the architect had to do was "graceful expression".

The role of Librarian in planning comes to stay gradually and it has been summed by Ellsworth, "Times have changed, today the librarian and a planning committee control the early stages of planning. They write the programme and lay down the description of the functions the building is to serve. The architect's task is to create a building that will perform the functions described in the programme." We find a lot of literature as to the procedures of planning, librarian's duties towards planning etc. Thus, we can conclude with Tauber and Wilson, "He should work closely with the building committee in preparing specification and should pay particular attention to such matters as the functions of the various rooms, the relationships among them, the probable use of the building and its supervision, the flexibility of its interior, provisions for future expansion and probable cost of operation".

B. PLANNING PRINCIPLES

1. Elementary Needs

For librarians, as guiding lines, while participating in building planning, some principles have been evolved. These lay down objectives of the university library in the context of various educational patterns. In 1888, Talbot Williams states, "A model library will discharge three offices ... it will store the books in absolute safety from fire in accessible manner, with light, air and an average temperature and with provision for indefinite expansion; it will provide space and room for rendering the books, accessible to readers by adequate library administration; and lastly, it will furnish all classes of readers with the accommodation they demand, varying from the five minutes reading of the casual reader to the years of silent investigation by the historian." It is remarkable that at so early date, we had such a sublime and general statement of library building objectives applicable for all times.

2. Soule's ten Principles

In 1897 Soule, in a library brochure laid emphasis upon ten points where he emphasized library's specific purposes, interior planning, adaptability, simplicity of decoration, economical administration and natural light. In 1926 Mauran wrote, "Taking into account the practical uses of the modern library, it is readily seen that it needs a building planned from the inside not from without, dictated by convenience and not by taste, no matter how good."

3. Githen and Wheeler :

Githen and Wheeler in their classical work laid down thirty-three principles for planning a library building. Some of those are: "A satisfactory library building can be evolved only through careful, joint study on the part of the architect, the librarian, and the building committee of the Library Board ... Many errors may be prevented by the appointment at an early date of a competent librarian, if the library does not have one ... the location of the library should attract and serve the greatest possible number of people ... The planning of the interior of the building as to important rooms and their relationship and arrangement is necessary before the exterior is designed ..."

These principle are not original contribution of Githen and wheeler, but those are the general principles that could establish at the time of their writing.

4. Gilbert Underwood :

Gilbert Underwood relates that, "I would study it first to make it the most perfect machine for its job. I would try to think of its functioning fifty or thousand years from now. Then I would study its facades to tall honestly the story of the plan on the outside. It would not hang a 'style' on it; I would create the style out of function and materials. When it was completed I would expect it to be a building in which the complex techniques of modern library service could function smoothly and efficiently, and which would suggest in its very structure something of the beauty of the cultural heritage which library services exists to preserve and pass on.[2]

5. Metcalf :

In 1945, K.D. Metcalf feels, "that librarian should base library building plans and also should acquire capability. The impact of world war II brought the university and the federal government closer together than ever before." This relation affected in the type of students attracted to the universities; in teaching methods and research services; and the emphasis they placed upon international problems and world understanding. The present functions of a university can be summed up as the conservations of knowledge and ideas; teaching; research; publication; extension and service; and interpretation. The libraries, for their very existence, have directed their activities towards the meeting of these ends through various means. To make democracy effective, through mass education, it is observed, "A rapid growth in number of students; expansion of curricula, involving introduction of new specialized courses, teaching departments and institutes as well as professional schools; introduction of methods of teaching; and an increased emphasis upon research."

6. Library Responsibilities :

Thus, libraries are expected to house more extensive book collection; to provide reading rooms or separate libraries for increased number of undergraduates; to provide for individual study and research facilities for more graduate students and faculty members; to equip themselves with special apparatus for careful preservation and reproduction of materials; and to have additional work space and other accommodation for larger library staff. This reasons out the changing patterns in the following pages.

C. ARCHITECTURE-LIBRARY BUILDING :

"From the middle of the nineteenth century to 1931, there was steady evaluation of the research library with various book storage arrangements and large monumental reading rooms." All these buildings were designed to fit one of the traditional architectural styles i.e., Gothic, Greek, Romanesque or Georgian. In the following paragraphs, the patterns of these architectural styles are briefly described.

1. Gothic :

"The basic principles of the Gothic styles were first, the concentration of thrusts upon isolated points of support, a method adopted by the late Romanesque designers in their substitution of groined for barrel vaults; and second, balanced thursts ... The natural corollaries, whose development was faced through the application of those two principles were ribbed vaulting and the pointed arch." We find further developing stages of this style termed as Early Pointed Period (1160 - 1275), Middle Pointed Period (1275 – 1375), etc. "Gothic architecture has in all its phases in almost all its local expressions certain constant characteristics. It has been termed as style of continuous growth and freedom."

2. Greek :

About Greek architecture we find that, "Greek architecture was entirely a matter of uprights and horizontal; of columns and walls supporting beams ... Greek architecture like art is sublimely beautiful because it is like nature." Greek style further developed into Doric, Ionic and Corinthian styles.

3. Romanesque :

"This architecture primarily based upon Roman, varying in each province according to the exigencies of climate, and the registration of racial characteristics in decorative form and structural inventiveness, is known under the generic title Romanesque style."

With Romans the building of a great monument comprised two distinct operations; first, the fabrication of the ossature or core; and secondly, the envelop or decoration which was an independent of the construction as clothing is independent of man.

4. Two works of Labrouste and the British Museum :

Turning to the actual patterns of early university library buildings we find that "The three types of libraries represented by the two works of Labrouste and the British Museum, furnished the patterns for most of the large libraries of the late nineteenth and early twentieth century. To the type of St Genieve belonged to the library of the University of Chicago (1910). To the type of Bibliotheque National Library with a reading room parallel or perpendicular to the stacks, belonged to the Widner Memorial Library, Harvard the Toronto University Library and many other university libraries. To the type of the British Museum i.e. with a circular reading room surrounded by the book-stacks and lighted by high windows or skylights, belonged to the Columbia University Library, New York (1897).

5. John Hopkins University Library Pattern :

A special type of architectural style evolved for John Hopkins University, Baltimore in 1914, became a pattern for repetition. In this pattern, we find a special emphasis was laid upon affording the small groups of advance students working in classes in the building (i.e., seminar groups).

6. Functional Pattern :

The pattern need for logical expression in the evolution of the functional requirements of the plans arose in the end of the third decade of the 20th century. Hitherto, the libraries were treated in the modernized classic tradition, or in the general style of collegiate Gothic architecture adopted for the group.

7. Divisional Pattern :

Some libraries with multi-storeyed buildings organised themselves with a divisional pattern. Here, every floor is self-sufficient with a stack hall, reading hall, research cubicles, seminar rooms etc. and each floor is allotted to one sector of knowledge i.e., Social Sciences, Humanities and Pure Sciences, or a floor for undergraduates.

8. Modular Pattern :

The latest development in the field of university library buildings is modular pattern. The changing objectives of the university education vis-a-vis library, made even relatively new buildings, with fixed functional structure, obsolete. With this pattern, the libraries have achieved adaptability to the changing needs and provided for future expansion without any architectural disturbance. Since 1945, the main patterns found are variation in the modules with progress in building engineering techniques. It has been a variation from 18' module to 24' module.

D. LIBRARY BUILDING: EXTERNAL

For a long period, libraries were housed in a centrally located hall, where books could be stored with some space for consultation. The earliest attempts to design a library in the modern sense was a proposal by Leopold delay Santa dating 1816 separate rooms, it is stated not these, were proposed by him for staff, readers and books. However, his plans could never be realized.

1. Location

11. Central :

The library was being provided, for sometime, a central location due to its academic functions and architectural beauty. There had been one opinion in favour of central location. "A good library building unsatisfactorily located is less desirable than an unsatisfactory library building having a good location." The site should be large enough to accommodate the present building and admit of future expansion. The University of Illinois has usually been quoted as an example of an institution which carefully retained open space for future units of the library.

12. Periphery :

"A centrally-located building though more accessible could only meet the educational requirements by being easily accessible, at the outset, a much larger building than required. A building which would be flexible enough to adequately meet expansion needs would more reasonably be errected in sections over a period of time, and a location near the periphery of the campus, therefore be favoured."

Thus, the main considerations evolved for site, with respect to changing objectives of university education have been settled as, a site of sufficient size, to provide space for a library building planned not only to suit needs of the present, but capable of expansion to meet such conditions as may develop in future.

13. Rational View :

"It should be near the lecture hall or halls, but not necessarily in the geographical centre of the campus. The building should not be too near to a main highway with its distracting influences nor near a music hall of an athletic field.

2. Shape-patterns

21. Circular :

In 1852, Panizzi developed the circular reading room without any separate stack room, into a large plan with book rooms surrounding the reading hall. This plan was used first in British Museum, repeated at Library of Congress. The circular shape was copied by the architects e.g. at columbia University, New York (1897), Leeds University (1936). The circular shape was beautiful from architectural view-points but it could not meet the new objectives of expansion and adaptability.

22. Greek Cross :

A centralized square or octagonal reading room around which the other elements of the library distributed, making a ground plan of Greek Cross, usually surmounted by domes became popular in the beginning of the 20th century. This pattern is available with e.g. John Hopkin University Library (1914), Baltimore, Cambridge University Library (1964) England, Massachusetts Institute of Technology Library (1953) Mass. The domed building could meet needs for flexibility and expansion least successfully, and reading rooms often distributed by traffic.

23. Linear-plan patterns

23.1 Angular-L.T.U. & I Shapes :

From Kansas (1924), an angular arrangement of two wings, one containing the reading rooms, the other storage element, making external shape of l or T, sometimes, if other wings added to form I or U became popular. Angular shapes have been found best solutions for design problems, so we find it repeated at e. g., Dayton (1928), North Western University (1929), Atlanta (1932), Arizona Library (1927) in the angular plans provided a new shape 'E'. This pattern has been found most adopt to expansion and flexibility. The University of Southern California, while making an attempt in the angular plan to provide lawns inside the building for loud discussions on readings, put forth a new shape of 'H'. This shape, admitting of good natural light has been very popular.

24. Rectangular :

From Emory University Library (1926), we have a rectangular shape pattern. In this shape, This is considered to be the most economical pattern and we have this repeated with e.g. University of Maryland, Ohio (1931), Howard (1935), Temple University (1936), Utah (1936) and Drew University (1938). Howard (1938). This linear rectangular shape with modifications and having multi-storeyed buildings is the pattern popular during present-day times.

25. Factory type :

The library of Michigan University (1920) provided a shape pattern termed as American factory type. This pattern did not become popular and remained lonely with a repetition elsewhere.

26. Functional :

Wayne University Library revolted against this shape pattern and paved grounds for consideration of functions alone. The external shape in the pattern is to be dictated by functions arranged internally i.e., planning from within than without.

27. To sum up :

From this study of external shape patterns of university library buildings, the following characteristics are discernible :

1. The existence of a variety of external shape patterns dictated aesthetic by idealistic, structural economy and functional reasons. Nevertheless, shapes are available to suit the site.
2. There is no chronological sequence in the occurrence of these patterns. It is form that various shape patterns, origination on the basis of the difficulties experienced. The later patterns could not oust the earlier instead allowed their repetition, side by side their own.
3. The changing moods and modes of the university education, architectural styles and planning procedure are reflected here. In the words of Ellsworth, during the post second world war, university libraries differed so widely from one another in concept of service, thus revealing basic differences in the universities themselves. The similarity of the older buildings was caused by the state of the building technology of that time, the domination of rigid concept of architectural style, and the fact that the librarians had little to say about the planing of librarians.

E. LIBRARY BUILDING :INTERNAL

1. Readers' Activities :

Unti' the last half of the nineteenth century, internally, the pattern of university library had been simple. The aims being limited, to serve readers for reference and to accommodate books, shelves combined with desks for reading and writing were found sufficient e.g. Trinity Hall College Library.

11. Stall system :

To accommodate more users in the library and increased book stock due to advent of rotary press, stall system was introduced. It consists of double sided book case, originally with two shelves and more, one above the other, and a sloping reading shelf below for reading in sitting position e. g. In Oxford Colleges (i.e. Merton, Jesus, St. John's Trinity (1620), Lincoln (16590 and queens (1696)

12. Verticle stacks vs reading Rooms :

In the middle of 19th century, the problem of supplying many books to many readers asked for a bigger building. This was solved by creating a verticle relationship in-between stacks and reading rooms. Reading room in this pattern usually enjoyed day light from above e.g. University of Chicago Library (1910), Leeds University (1936), Swansea University collage library (1937), Shefield University library (1959) and further observed in 1945 at Texas, Rochester, Enoch Pratt, Caen, Saarbrucken, Hamburg, Yale, Mexico and Manchester.

13. Central reading Rooms :

"Central reading room surrounded by stacks e. g. Columbia university library, new York (1897)......" , University of leeds, Nebraska, Colorado, Liverpool and University College London. This pattern gave disadvantage to frequent disturbance to readers.

14. Rear Book Stack Front Reading Room :

Opposite to this arrangement was a central stack hall surrounded with reading rooms. This pattern developed at a time when daylight for book-stacks became unessential. In this arrangement, makes a building compact but retards the usual needed expansion of stacks. First founded at John Hopkins University, Baltimore (1914) (with inner courtyard), and repeated at columbia university (Butler library) (1935), New Bodleian library oxford (1940), Moscow University, U S S R (1953), University of Maryland, U S A (1957).

15. Tower-like stack-pattern :

At some university libraries, we find books stacks in the form of a tower. The tower lands itself to castrating subject reading rooms at different levels. Examples for this pattern are university of Rochester (1930), fisk university (1931), Pittsburgh university (1936), Cambridge University (1934), London University (1937), Ghent University (1940), University of Saar, Saarbruoken (1984).

16. Dispersed :

The new modular pattern has stacks and reading rooms dispersed in the building e. g. Wayne, Iowa, Michigan, Rutgers.... ..... Appendix).

2. SPACE FOR MATERIAL

21. Books - Open Access :

Till 1930s, mostly the access to books was not direct. The stacks were closed and were controlled by attendants at the desk. The reasons given in favour of closed access were, economy in keeping shelves in order, convince to researchers and minimum reliance on tricky classification system. "It is said that looking in vain for a book that someday want to read. I submit that this procedure, of compulsory or even normal, is an uncivil waste of readers' time and reputation of exact scholarship. However, in spite of this opposition, in the early 1930s and later, traditional concept of the book stacks for storage of books has given way to the pattern that would permit other activates carried out in that area.

22. Periodical Room :

A separate periodical room has its origin with a rapid growth of periodical literature since the beginning of this century, as it required a special handling for storage and service. For sometime, a separate Iowa, Saarbucken, caen, Michigan, for instance) but, in others the periodicals are merged with the subject literature (Colorado and Nebraska).

3. NEW CONCEPTS

31. Reproduction Laboratories

Research libraries are finding it essential to provide for one or all these work i. e. "Verifox for quick, inexpensive copying for use; photostacking when high quality work is necessary; are provided at chicago, Californian, M. I. T. Etc. less elaborate laboratories are found in almost all the university libraries.

32. Space for Readers :

There had been a lot of discussions as to how much space be provided for readers as compared to university enrolment. Tilton suggested that a library should provide seats for one-half of the total strength. Warner, while writing for C. H. University library, thought that a provision for 25% was reasonable. Gerculd increased this ratio to 30% as the minimum. Reece in 1952 summed up, "Norms have risen in a few decades from ten to fifty per cent. Brock in 1958 concluded, having examined the actual existing situation of eighty-seven libraries, that 25% was normal.

33. General Reference Room :

In earlier days, when reference functions got established,

the kinds of books listed in mudge were shelved and used under the guidance of reference staff. In the universities of Michigan, Columbia, Illinois and California, such a room was found to be used as a general reading room as well. "It is agreed after extensive discussions that there can no longer be a single definition of purpose, scope of size reference." Presently, in modular buildings, where the physical structure does not force a specific limitation on any one function, one finds a wide variation of layout for reference, depending on the conception held by the administration of individual library.

34. Reserve a Book Rooms :

These developed because of the urge to have at hand the books required frequently by students and the faculty. These are available at open (at Oberlin and Yale), closed at (Jowa and Illinois) books arranged on the shelves either under courses of study or the name of the professor. The abundance of packet books at low cost, lessened its utility. But the adoption of inductive teaching replacing the traditional ones, required in use a combination of one text book and many additional readings. This retained the idea of Reserve Book room in the university library. The principle of open access, however, has made it obligatory with the library enter to have separate rooms or have the collection marked and merged in the general stack.

35. Browsing Rooms-New Educational Concepts :

These were very popular in American university libraries during 1930s as a means of an incentive for reading contemporary books. The open shelf system since world war II has lessened the need for browsing collection.

36. Conference Rooms :

The idea of conference rooms is becoming popular since world war II, allowing students to study in groups. These are located usually adjacent to the reading rooms. At Iowa, the demand was so heavy that the library committee requested the library to start a system of scheduling the use of rooms to prevent certain groups form monopolizing their use.

37. Seminars :

The idea of providing seminars started in twenties continued in thirties. A need for studying and talking in the same room gave rise to a new pattern-a unit of two rooms called as a work room and a talk room. While making the seminar-continued books easily available, these were located near the stacks room collection. Their existence has been challenged, "These are not available to others while seminars are in session, have often proved wasteful."

38. Research Carrels :

By throwing open the libraries to all undergraduates, graduates, brought in disturbance to the serious readings of researchers and faculties. So, libraries have begun to have research carrels in the least disturbed areas of the library.

391. Auditorium :

Originally, the idea was developed with adult education, However, feeling library as soul of the university life auditoriums have been provided at the Lament, Florida etc. to provide life.

392. Audio-visual-use rooms :

The formal printed book transformed into microfilms, microcards, records, magnetic tape, slides, act., has placed responsibility upon the library for their preservation and use. Such a space now we find in all the university libraries.

393. Space for library staff :

3931. Processing space :

In the European university libraries, each operation in

processing is allotted a separate room and books are carried from room until released. But in U S A, Large open space is allotted to processing section.

394. Organizing Internally :

A lot of literature has been produced upon this aspect of the library building by librarians. This has been analysed and summed up by Thompson who makes three zones of the library while distributing various functions within the building i. e. Noisy, Talking and Quiet.

F. LIBRARY-BUILDING-HISTORY (U G C) INDIA

1. Up to Independence :

Till independence, we find a gloomy picture about university library buildings. University, all the libraries for quite a long period, housed their collection in a building never meant for experienced circle of librarians and architects, planning the future library building with better understanding. For this purpose, it is suggested that U G C should have a permanent wing of expert librarians, critically examining the library building plans coming for approval to U G C. This will be better it the expert opinion is provided at the initial levels of planning the university library buildings avoiding the architectural expenses for making the suggested changes at a later stage. Only then we can talk like Metcalf think it is fair to say that we are now getting about 50% more for our money. Ours is a poor country we cannot afford costly experiences to serve for hundred years, with new structures.

2

University Library System : Furniture And Equipment

1. GENERAL

A University library system devoted to the functions of education and research facilities cannot fulfil its functions till it has functional as well elegant library building furnished with compatible furniture items as also equipment in accordance with the use of new information technology to enhance efficiency of the Central Library and its wings-the departmental libraries as a unit. To increase efficiency, to reduce errors and to release the professional personnel from routine duties, a number of gadgets that have been successfully used in business and industry are available for use a modern university library system. No university library now-a-days can function in isolation. It has to cooperate not only with other university libraries within the country but also at global level with all the libraries being *member of the local area networks* (LAN) to wide area networks (WAN) and through these or directly to harness the boons of new information technology for the benefit of the learned clientele-students, undergraduates as well as postgraduates, research scholar and faculty members-through Internet, Ernet etc.

It is an important factor that if a university library is provided with elegant, cosy and practical furniture, its efficiency and popularity increases. The library users shall find themselves comfortable and find libraries the best work place for their research pursuits. Furniture and equipment play a vital role in presenting the library as an effective and impressive institutions to the clientele. Dr. Ranganathan, father of library science, states that the quality of furniture and equipment reflects the interest librarian as also university authorities take in the development of the university library system. Therefore, in the internal arrangement of the library building furniture and equipment demand top priority.

In this lesson reference will be available to all the items of furniture and equipment but description shall be delimited to such items that are exclusively useful for making the library functional and a practical laboratory for the researchers.

2. THE FURNITURE

A University Library needs for efficient functioning the following items of furniture for organisation and storage of reading material in traditional as also multi-media form:-

Shelving : There are many types of shelving available, including industrial shelving and application of the slotted angle variety. The modern trend in university libraries is towards the lighter, sturdy and more flexible types of shelving. Godrej, Allwyn and Vinar are three companies provide the steel rack units. Some libraries approach manufacturers provided when they are to furnish a new library building. However, here will shall concern overself to dimensions and material alone and the choice of suppliers is left to individual university librarians.

2·1 Steel Shelving are available and in use of heights 6', 7', 2', or 8', width is usually 3' and depth varies inbetween 8" – 12". The uprights are usually of steel sheet having a right angle bend at the back with a tubular front. Shelves are made with a turn up at the back to prevent books being pushed through. Shelves are adjustable to 1" height and panels can also be fitted. The shelving is usually in stove enamelled alive green or grey. The suppliers offer other colours also.

Wall shelving ranging from 6" height with 5 shelves to 9" high 6 shelves are also in fashion.

2·2 Book Cases with window panes- steel and wooden are also available in some of the university libraries developed from a collage level to a university library. Some rare and out of print books are kept in book cases as also in steel almirahsunder lock and key. These book cases are usually 5" high 1" deep with four shelves fixed.

2·3 Wooden/Steel

The dimensions of double faced racks haven been standardized as 7" 3" heightx3" width and 18" depth, the shelves are usually adjustable at a 1" through the side strips. 18" depth is provided with a strip dividing and separating the reading material on each face. The strip is usually of 4" height. Some of the older universities having closed access to their reading material have wooden shelves and wooden almirahs as well for the shelving of books in the stackhall. Uprights available are 37" to 90" x depth 8" to 18" x shelf length is mostly 36" but at times 36" length of shelf-units is also marketed.

2·3 Movable Shelving

These are usually made of timber. The steel rail is fitted to timber bearers which are fixed to the surface of the floot not into it. Standard sizes vary 70" – 91" to build up-right height, shelf-depth varies from 12" – 16" Breadth varies 35" – 47"

There are movable steel shelves also. Standard dimensions are 3" wide, 7" – 12" deep, height from 7" – 3" to 10" – 6" These are usually double faced with partitions in the middle of the depth through stripes. The shelves can either be braced or fitted with solid backs.

2·4 Shelf-Equipment

(a) Tier Guides : metal size varies 3"× 1/4" to 12"x4" Tier guides in plastic are supplied by Library Equipment Service in various sizes.

Book Cases : Book case units of the size range 30" height *x* 12" deep *x* 281/2" width to 3' – 6" high x 2' – 10" wide x 14" deep, three adjustable shelves with sliding glass doors are also available with Vinar and Godrej.

2·5 Periodical Racks

48" long *x* 70 ½" high *x* 15" deep in wood steel and four shelves with graded heights $14^1/_2$. 13" *x* and two of 12" each; below the display shelves there is cupboard space with sliding doors. Besides these some manufactures are marketing freestanding racks-for 50 periodicals-25 each side. or 72 periodicals - 36 each side or 108 periodicals - 54 each side.

2·6 Newspaper Stands

With perspex-fronted divisions, standard size B36" × 12½ D × 43" high. Again another variety with dimensions 6" x3" wide section units with 5 divisions are also marketed.

2·7 Desk Book Stands and Book Rests

Steel book rack 15" long × 12" high × 8½" deep with 10 compartments each 1" wide.

Book Stand 1" – 5½" long 8" deep

Table book troughs of dimensions :

2" long × 10¼" deep × 8½" high

2 or 3" long × 10¼" deep × 71½" high

Metal desk stand with 6 divisions. Height 12" × width 15" × 8" depth.

2·8 Atlas and Encyclopaedia Stand

(a) Atlas Stand with six storage shelves, five of which can be pulled outwords: 39" × 30" × 19½".

Atlas and folio stands : Sloping six shelves, of which five are sliding, dimensions are 3" – 3½" high × 2" – 6" wide × 1" – 7" deep.

(b) **Dictionary Stand :** with shelf and sloping top. Made in steel sheet/oakwood of dimensions 3" – 5" high × 1" – 9" length × 1" 4" deep.

(c) **Atlas cases** with slightly sloped top fitted with ledge and six shelves. The top five shelves pull out. The case is with dimensions 3" 5" high × 2" 6" wide × 1" 7" deep.

2·9·1 Chairs

(a) Easy : Three types of easy chairs are available in a variety of models estimated as one score.

(b) Stacking/Folding: Folding and seven types of steel stacking chairs.

(c) Adjustable : Twenty one models are available.

(d) Polypropylene : linking and stacking chairs are available.

For university libraries in India Panicking Road, Delhi provides the best choice of chairs. Further the manufacturers take contact to fabricate and manufacture chairs according to the dimensions and choice of material by University Librarian to furnish their lounge, crushhslls, reading rooms, administrative offices of the library with elegant, stout and durable chairs. The height is the always 2" to seat.

2·9·2 Tables

In Indian University libraries, we find a variety of tables for users when they wait in a lounge or for the use of users and to conduct official work efficiently in the office and for different levels of office staff as well as professionals.

(a) Readers' Tables : (i) Single faced with dimensions :

2' × 3" × 6"

H W L

(ii) Double Faced : 2' × 4' × 6' / 2' × 4' × 8'
H W L H W L

(iii) 4' × 5' × 2' again for 4 users double faced seating
W L H

four readers with partitions 5' × 5' × 2'
W L H

(iv) 4' × 6' or 2' Up stand and top covered.
W D H

(b) Periodical Tables with display provision having dimensions 5" × 5" in the centre 9" area used to make both sides display rack with three shelves.

(c) Executive Tables : Tables for the Deputy Librarians as well as Chief Librarians. We also need tables for Assistant Librarians. All these tables may be of such a size that in case Librarian eight persons may be accommodated on three sides, the main side for the librarian 5' × 9' × 2'.
W L H

Similarly to accommodate six persons on the table 4' × 6' × 2' and for others it can be a table of the
W L H

size $2\frac{1}{2}$' × 5' × 2'. For typist we need a table
W L H

2' × 4' × 2'.
W L H

This furniture can be wooden with teak-board top or steel from a standard company such as Godrej, Vinar, Alwyn etc.

2·9·3. Browsing Room Cony Furniture

In browsing room we need armless sofa chairs around a round shaped central table to accommodate 3 – 4 units of 5 – 6 readers. We also need in this area elegant benches. We need benches in the stack area to accommodate displaced books so that being placed on floor may not get worn-torn.

2·9·4. Research Scholars' Carrel

We need furnishing of cubides and project room with adequate furniture: easy chair, office chair, table with two armless chairs.

2·9·5 For the seminar room we need such units of tables that can be joined to make an oval shape circle to accommodate up to 50 persons fitted with ten speakers, sound system microphones etc. To the walls there must be provision of seventy chairs to accommodate participants in discussions or audience in lectures. This room can be used for orientation talks in the beginning of the sessions to orientate newly admitted students.

3. ALLIED EQUIPMENT TO FURNITURE

(a) Catalouge Cabinets

Units of 24 drawers each. The unit be added as per requirements of the size of the book stock and Catalogue card stock.

This is to be replaced during the modern time by computer aided database system with terminals spread over the entire library. The basis problem with this application is the power load-shedding due to which library catalogue shall be unavailable for public use. Therefore public catalogue for the use of students, researchers and faculty members in traditional form as a duplicate approach is a must till India becomes independent in energy (power) requirements for industrial and other uses.

(b) Lighting (Desk)

Ceiling lights in a University Library are frequently available but there is a range of mobile working lights and bench lights (fluorescent). Fluorescent desk lamps-these can be placed on working surfaces or secured to wall. The reflector rotates and pivots about the stem. The shaft height is 19" and the length of shade unit is 28" A range of adjustable desk and table lamps are available in the market of standard makes.

(c) Cupboards, Locker and Wardrobes

Most of the furniture listed in furniture section is adaptable, cupboards can be fitted to wall to take lateral filing for stationary storage. Many a models of cupboards can be fitted with bookcases. These are other similar utility articles from the viewpoint of keeping users property secure with an attendant. Cupboards are unhelpful because bigger articles cannot kept there. Property counter fitted with elegant shelves and token system can be the best alternative arrangement.

(d) Ladders and Stools

Safety the most important feature of any height aid. All ladders and stools being marketed by manufacturers are fabricated with safety and elegance viewpoint. The model of ladders available are two steps for height 79" and five steps are suitable up to for level up to 107".

A variety of folding aluminium ladders, the most suitable for library purposes are also available, these are of 2, 4 and 7 treads models.

Another alternative is *step stools* having 2 or 3 trade that are also manufactured from multipurpose angles and are useful for university libraries. A wide range of shelf ladders, tubular safety ladders and steps, platform steps all suitable for library use are obtainable from the furnishers. A 714" height aid-stool which rolls at a light-touch and stops the instant weight is applied. Platform has a rubber safety tread and there is an all round rubber bumper protection. A similar type equipment is available of 14" height.

(e) Trolleys

Office or table trolleys with suntica tops also named as mobile display trucks-four to six shelves finished in coca-cola or light silver oak as per internal colour of library walls with dimensions width 41" depth 18" height 46" distance between sinuses 9½ another model of two upper shelves on both sides sloped, bottom shelf flat for large books-dimensions-Height 86" width 17" or it can be got fabricated as per requirement of the library *i.e.* two or three pieces at each floor of the University library to transport issued books returned/books disturbed in the shelving area being transported for resolving or it may be books processed and completed in the technical section to be transported for display or their merger into the shelved books. Dimensions can be varied when these are got manufactured by contract. Trclleys are also available known as all purpose trolley suitable for machine room equipment transportation or postal distribution trolley-two *x* wells for easy stair levels negotiations-two detachable frames filled with canvas bags each with nine vertical divisions and metal indicator frames. Extra frames are also made available with bottom trays. The finishers also make available carton trolley which is equipped with an inclined hinged ramp attached to its lower tray. This is designed to assist operators in handling in to position the heavy cartons transportation from one section to another. The top surface can also be put to use.

(f) Hat, Coat and Umbrella Stand

Now-a-days, the libraries are found air-conditioned and accessories with library employees and user require their deposit at the entrance. Same is the case with umbrellas to ward off sunshine or cains. These stands if kept at the entrance of the library with the staff then the library can be saved from dust and dirt. At the entrance to the compute room we need shoe racks, so that dust does not create virus to computer hardware.

(g) Waste Paper Bins

Every stationer stock this most useful piece of a university library equipment. The librarians must acquire these annually as per their requirement. These if provided at frequent points in different sections help upkeep of the library neat and clean. Daily disposal of intake shall keep than usable.

4. DISPLAY, LABELLING, LETTERING AND REPAIR EQUIPMENT

4·1 For display of reading material-display stand 35½" × 23½" with rubber buffers fitted to the sides. It can be floor stand complete with two or four panels. Standard dimensions : Height 57", panels 35½ × 23½, a two panel model similarly there can be with Height 58¼" panel sizes 13" wide and 22" high, floor space 16" square.

There can be revolving display stands for books mainly for table use with different panel size-selections as per requirements, height 33" In case display panels are to be fixed in the walls-display brackets for display of books are also available in different sizes and material.

4.2 Periodical Display Covers and Binders

These are available with the stationers at Nai Sarak, Delhi in plastic fitted transparencies in different sizes ranging from 10" × 7" to 15¼" × 10¼" sizes. These are being fabricated and marketed keeping in view the requirements of periodical sections of libraries. The suppliers advertise their products as standard sizes. Magazine covers in cloth, half-bound with title of front transparent magazine covers, journal binders and newspaper covers are made to order. Ready-made display binders are made available in the sizes quarto, A4. Dammy, King size, Royal size etc. Similarly display pocket transparent to hold books and magazine are also available for use in libraries with the Delhi stationers.

4·3. Book Protection

Self-adhesive transparent PVC is available in rolls of 22¼ yds at width from 8½ × 38", similarly another standard lengths are 10, 25, 50 yds and width of 9" × 10", 13" and 18: Three types of self-adhesive materials being marketed are Transparent seal, transparent sheen and Pe Ve cealea thicker version) in different lengths and standard width sizes.

4.4. Book Coverings, Non-Adhesive

These are available in rolls of 50 yards in width sizes of 9", 12" or 15" Polythene books covers in three sizes : 9", 16" for books up to 7" spines ; 11" × 18" for books up to 9" spines; 13" × 20" for books up to 11" spines. Book slaving rolls are also available in sizes 9" to 12" width, again 7" to 11½ size. These are available in varied colours in rolls of 40" width. It is suitable for all forms of immediate reinforced protection and printing by letter press or lithography.

4.5 DOCUMENT BINDING AND REPAIR :

(a) Thirma-bind that binds up to 4" thickness for sheets size 15".

(b) Cloth edge binding tapes available in white, red, blue or green in ½ ,½ width and 36 yards length.

(c) Paper welding machine binds sheets of up to 11½" in lenght to a total thickness of ½". There is equipment for threadless binding. The standard threadless hand operated binder complete with 6" clamping bar assembly side and flat aligners. The machine takes thickness up to and sizes up to 20" A number of binding solutions and gazes are also available.

(d) Plastic ring binding is available in a wide range of styles, diameters and colours. Other rangers of bindings incorporate 6 styles of 12 diameters in 7 colours together with an extensive selection of covers and loose-leaf metal ring binders.

Independent punches and binder also combined ones are available as well.

(e) **Embossing Machines :** Hand operated embossing machines supplied with 54 as also with 90 characters as per requirement and demand. A wide range of printing and embossing machines with library application are being market. These point or overpoint, automatically ejects items up to 16" width are hand/electrically operated.

(f) **Laminators :** A range of dry mounting and laminating equipment that can take a maximum mount size of 56" heat sealing film is available in 40" width. Sheet material is available in pockets.

(g) **Labelling Machine :** Label makers are available both left and right hand operation 1/4 , 3/8 or tapes in many a colours are available. The small machine (1/2" dia!) the larger 3/8 dial. Dials are snap-on and interchangeable, and additional dials with tape of the appropriate width are available. There are hand embossing machines available to produce round or square ended tapes. Tapes come in 1/4" ,3/8 or 1/2" width in varied colours with various matt or glossy finishes. Lengths or 72", 120" or 144" are available in boxes of six. A slightly different piece of labelling equipment is made known as weber tab on stencil for continuous making. Particular library application on stencil for continuous making. Particular library application would be where the name of the library or firm has to be marked on all documents. The marking system machines giving, 5 lines of lettering 32 (typing characters wide another model giving output of 24 lines deep 50 characters wide. The libeller is self-inking and stencil can be typed or written or to produce a clear copy.

(h) **Stylus (Electric) :** It is available with two inter-change-able writing points, one for medium, one for fine lines, Tarns foils for use with this is also available in rolls of french lengths.

A similar stylus is stocked and transfer paper is also supplied by a few firms for a particular use on PVC bank jackets.

(1) Lettering : Dry Transfer System

A variety of modern type faces are available in Black White red, yellow or blue colours. Technical symbols are also available. The yellow have guidelines and the backing sheets can be replaced on unused letters.

Fingerprint characters are sold in strips in a older containing upper and lower case characters. Each strap has vertical and horizontal control grid for easy positioning. Coloured and special sheets are also available in the market.

Trains letters-water slide transfers which stick to flat surface including glass. Letters come in different at sizes from ½" to 5½",

Printmachine - a hand printing process using firefly movable type in conjunction with a specially designed frame and slide different type faces are available in 70 sizes and in available in 8 colours. Handpiece and spacing and spacing bars-a table board and extension rule suitable for use with large type faces.

All these are stationery, press and printing them not designed for libraries. These are to be purchased keeping in view library work and due adjustments can be made accordingly.

The items of equipment in section 3 and 4 are the rwise used by people in there homes and offices and in the by the sophisticate population and are available for libraries as well. For modification, if any manufactures can be contacted and libraries can be equipped with modern gadgets. However, the main problem is the finance that is being provided to the state University library. The books grants by U. G. C. are so small so are the books, Grants forms state government, the standard formula of 20% of the grant on staff and 5% on stacks is not being followed by most of the university libraries in India.

5. BOOK HANDLING AND IN CREMATION RETRIEVAL

5.1 Vertical card filing

There is a housing system for single or multi-cards of any sizes- Houses groups of sets of tabulating punched card-plates for groups selection. There is a special version of this housing unit holding tabulating pushed cards for individuals selection. The main Divider ensures that the visible section of the card remains constant. Cabinets are available on castorbased for protoblast.

5.2 Visible Record Equipment

Deep trays for card sizes 5" × 3", 6" × 4" , 8" × 5", 10" × 6", 12" × 6" (having 8, 12 or 16 trays.) similar card sizes and trays as also housing 8" × 6" cards, with interlocking pockets are available in the marked. A wide range of cabinets of 5" × 3" (standard catalogue cards' size) to 12" × 10" sized cards with 8 to 20 trays are readily available in the market.

Rendngton Rand Ltd. as well as Godrej Ltd. are catering to needs regarding KARDEX cabinets for card sizes fros 6" × 4" to 11" × 9" from 8 to 13 trays capacity from 57 to 77 pockets per glide (descending on card size) are reading available with them.

5.3. Book Units

Units for card sizes 6" × 4" and 8" × 5" for 50 or 100 pockets are available in the market. there are book units in 2 or 4 folds,3 lengths, holding from 60 to 320, 6" × 4" cards 50 to 300, 8" × 5" cards and 72 or 112, 10" × 6" cards are also available. Made in various size units with capacity from 50 cards onwards are manufactured to order. Books and single panels housing from 30 to 100 records are available. Binders are also available.

5.4 Strip Index

Are available in 12" × 22" high reference panels as wall bracket units, desks or rotary stands. There are strip index systems available on rotary stands (darrying up to 50 double sided panels as desk panels (double sided) or (single sided wall panel)

5.5 Accession Registers

These consist of multi-ring binders with 11" × 14" sheets ruled and headed for accessioning books.

There is space approximately for 5000 entries and extra sheets if desired can be added. Larger binder for 10,500 entries is also available.

5.6 Book conveyors

These are normally made to special requirements and photographs and illustrations can be collected form professional literature as well as dears list that is published from U. S. A. For the people of all walks.

5.7 Charging System :

5.7.1 Manual

Included in this section are readers tickets, book cards and pockets, date labels, issue trays, book issue cards, date, month and division guides for use in issue trys: data labels. Firms supplying these include :

1. Standard Library service,
2. Mehra Library Service, Bahadurgarh Road, Delhi. Dimensions of Items :
   (a) *Readers Tickets* : The usual size is 3" × 2" or 3½" × 2" o top and sides in manila or coloured including up to four lines of printing.
   (b) *Book Cards* : ruled for heading and/or date in sizes form 3" × 1½" to 4" × 2½" Available in buff or colours.
   (c) *Book Pockets* : for use with above book cards.
   (d) *Data Labels* : gummed and ungummed. A few suppliers

supply a combined book pocket and date label. These items are of stationery x types. Most of the universities have their own university proses,, bindaries combined with them, therefore stationery is prepared by the university press as also printing work and binding work is done by the university press as also printing work and binding work is done by the university bindaries.

5.7.2 Mechanical

The equipment included in this section does not include microfilm cameras, which as the illustrations show, can also be used for book charging.

(a) *Bookmatic machine* : This makes the use of embossed plastic cards and a recording machine for date in printing.

(b) *Paramount cards* : suitable for use with book charging cameras. A few companies have circulated their wtite-up-a useful introductory paper on the whole operation of photo-charging and the application of paramount cards in the library.

(c) *Microfilm Equipment Company* : This company marketed in 1967 two magic eye cameras which become very popular throughout the world libraries as also in betting shops. The library application of the cameras are append and the manufacturers are working on these adaptations. There are two models the smaller magic eye the larger model.

(d) *Remington Rand Ltd* : Photocharger camera model BA/4-16. The image registered is 14 times reduced, the loading imagine gives a capacity of 3500 exposures. The machine includes 2 cassets. The machine is of Swedish origin. Remington Rand Ltd. Offers a processing service for a small additional cost.

5.8 NUMBERING AND DATING MACHINES

Hand numbering machines and automatic type-high numbering

machines and daters as also electric numbering and dating machines are also available.

5.9.1 Microfilm Equipment

(a) Cameras : Japanese Dea Graph range of cameras are being used by libraries. These are useful for microfilming comments up to 52" × 38" with reductions to 1.24 on 35mm film. A 16 mm adapter kit is also available as an enlarging head for up to 30x. Some models incorporate a vertically adjusting copy-toward allowing books up to 4" thick to be photographed.

A microfilm technique, firat available in U. S. A. Alone evolved by the national cash register Co. the technique achieves reduction up to 40,000 = 1. Consultation is by micro-image viewer which uses film transparencies of 3" × 5". The PMC = press converse microfilm into micro-images on a photochromic coatings with a high resolution and no grain. Images can be erased and recorded if correction are are necessary. After master film transparencies have been made on special material, low cost duplication can be made for use with appropriate viewers.

(b) Viewers : The alliance table reader : it incorporates : magnification ration of 7x or 16x; Screen size 16" × $10^1/_3$ models with stand are also available.

Kodak Ltd. – Marketed Recorded compact reader model 16/29. Designed for desk-top viewing of 16mm. microfilm on 100' ceel with screen size 9 1/2" x 12 1/2" Recorded archival reader. Primarily for 35 mm film but also allows for 16mm viewing. Magnifications of 24x and 12x.

Recordek unitised film reader model 6 b ; suitable for 3" × 5" cards, viewing screen 9" × 10½ magnification 23x.

Recorded unitised film reader model PK 1023 ; suitable for viewing microfilm cards up to 5"× 8"; screen 10½ × 12½ manifestoing 1 Ex or 23 x.

(c) combined camera and viewer : This consists of a

microfilm, camera suitable for b or 16mm film of documents of maximum 11 width. The reduction factor is 1 : 24 or 1 : 37. The reader anlages to 24 or 37x.

(d) Reader-Printers, Developers and enlargers : Electrostatic enlarger printer, prints from 8 to 16 enlargements of 35 mm micro films, card mounted or reel type. Positive image poisoning and fine focusing are facilitated by an inverted right reading machine projected in a viewing an object.

3 sheet sizes of copy paper are accommodated in the 8½" × 11" to 18" × 24" range. Machine is given on rent by the dealer.

5.9.2. Accessories

Include; Aperture cards, micro-card adapters, microfilm hand mounter for 35mm film; the 16mm mounter and semiautomatic optical mounter automatic aperture card feed, capacity 100 cards ; roll film input for 16 and 35mm ; card developer card printer etc. are marketed by manufacture and some of the university libraries purchase them.

5.9.3. Projectors

Among these are 2500/300 watt tarns former model with 5" × 7" viewing field; 500 watt overhead projector with tilting head, filed size 10" × 10"; size and films trip projectors; diascopies; Epidiascope to take 3¼" square slides the instrument can also project 2" × 2¼" square slides as well as positives on 35mm. strip film by means of attachments ; portable projector suitable ; for meetings auditorium size projector producing an image 20" × 20" are the variety marketed and some of the acquired by universality library system for the use of there faculty.

5.9.4. Information Retrieval systems

(a) *Feature card scanner* : Accepts feature cards or opacities 2,500 or 5,000 items; and scan them at a rate of 800 positions per second. It generates impales which may be fed into other equipment such as computers or teleprinters.

(b) *Feature card calculator* : which accepts from the scanner and carries out simple mathematic operations upon them. It can add substrata and multiply also can be giver a second register with other facilities.

(c) *Interpreter* : it can scan, calculate and interpret the impulses from the scanner to activate a creed punch tape head, or an automatic type head, and enables the numerical information on the feature cards to be translated in to written or punnhced tape information.

(d) *Feature card scanner converter* : it is used to feed information into computers. The referred to here are of first and second generation computers. From here onwards the university libraries continued functioning with this equipment as frequent replacements were not possible with expanding acquisition we shift to the modern pcs both ATs on XTs. we continue with further description of 1) card selecting units - reading, punches and grievers, punch card counters tradition material still requiring replacement.

5.9.5. Card selecting units

(a) *Findex* : in making a selection of findex cards, the operator places batches of up to 750 cards at a time into the selector. Two guide rods are first run through the guide holes at the side of the front plate and locked in position. The steel selecting rods are then run through the holes in the front plate and right through all the cards run slack over the rods, those which have slots in the positions against the rods are permitted to drop the distance of ½" cards which have two or more adjacent positions alotted and have a slot of an inch or more on the card will not fall further than ½" because the guide rods which have been placed in the side of each card. A looking rod is positioned in one of the bottom row of holes to prevent the selected cards falling back, and the selector is reverted to the upright position. The cards may then be counted or raised by means of rod which is inserted through the slots provided at the tops of the cards. Substraction selection can also be effected. The sorter available are of two sizes; for 6" × 8" cards.

(b) *Fact-finder* : This is a system of french origin which oberates on edge-notched cards and electric vibrator. The cards have no pre-punched holes, which makes them stronger, , and notched in the usual way. When a pack of cards is to be sorted, and notched in the usual way. When a pack of card is to be sorted, bars. Are inserted horizontally at the bottom of the vibrator through marked holes. About two hundred care can be sorted at a time and these cards are placed on a container resting on the inserted bars. When this is made vibrate, the cards with notches corresponding to the bars drop down ; the operation is completed in three seconds. The machine and cards are available in university libraries in three sizes, for cards these are 3¼" × 7" (normal) giving 167 positions.

The cards are in two thicknesses : life (giving up to 30 operations) and long life for normal use in the library. There are 32 program bar positions for the small and medium seized machines, 4s for the large size. The manufacturers have supplied in different university libraries 16 programme bars for the small and medium machines and 24 for the large size, more are have also been purchased as per requirement by a few libraries. Reference tray together with two fixing rods are included in the system.

(c) Manisort card selector frame having a capacity of up to 500 cards has also been found in a few university libraries - in two sizes small (up to 8½") and large (up to 11¼"). These models are hand operated electrically operated franes are also available.

5.9.6 Reading units

Such as visire card reader, for use with feature cards - pervaded with alignment guides and operates from 200-250 volts at 6 watts have also been found in use in a few university found in use in few university libraries.

5.9.7. Data card punches and Groovers

This is an auxiliary to the machines as hand punch for single are for punching groups ; hand drill as well as lever punch ejected punches ; a range of automatic key punch 3 and verifiers were modifications for library usage, keyboard no teacher, Body data card punches hand and electrically operated etc., are available with most of the university libraries.

5.9.8. Punched card counters

In this three items for equipment are used: (i) A recording unit, (ii) A retrieval unit, and lii an electric typewriter/card punch which codes indexing information in to the machine language on which the system operates. The encoding system is such that any kind of numeric, alphabetic or alpha numeric indexing may be used there is no restriction on the number of indexing terms which may be given to a particular document. Should there be insufficient room to record the compete indexing information, the camera will automatically skip one or more frames to accommodate the index. This operation-indexing information feeding verification as well as indexing takes about 5 seconds 32 quarto sized pages are recorded on each foot of 35mm film which is used in 200 magazines. After development the real of film is stored. These can be seen in INS DOC old records. Retrieval process involves placing of reel-film on the retrieval unit and an optical scanner compares the binary coded infirmation on the film with that on the card at a speed of 6,400 pages per minute. As the two codes agree, the film transport stops and the document. Image appears on a screen where from a printout can be made. After search the film is rewound automatically. In addition to searching random in to selected subjects and to store a single document under several relevant subject headings.

6. DOCUMENT FILING AND STORAGE :

The stationery, furniture and equipment item that can be included under this heading are; (a) Box Files - of different sizes and made out of card or plastic boards ; (b) Circular Filling units - with circularities which accommodate upright liver arch files of any standard sizes ; (c) Continuous Stationery liver arch-quarto, fool cape, A4 of octave - in book form or loose ; Wallets - usually document wallets and ; Files - including registers of all sizes (e) filing accessories - include index tabbing, guides, indicator signals, title holders, title insert strips, labels, protectors and clips ; (f) lateral filling unit -open rock riling, with open fronts, cupboard doors. double folding doors, blinds or roller shutters of varied sizes such as 36¾" wide - × 76" high × 18" deep ; 6" – 4" high × 3" wide × 1"6" deep with five rows of lateral files and metal shutters etc. (g) letter Raokes - usually of fools cape size up to 5 ties ; also included are metal sorting rack, flexible mesh trays etc. (h) mobile and portable filing units - trolley units of height 29 1/2 " x width 13 1/4" 17" depth ; these take 30 fools cape or 40 quarto filing pockets ;

(1) Shelf filing – this method of storage is lateral filing but with shelf-dividers rather than suspension rails and is particularly suitable where a limited amount of information must be held under a large number of single classifications,. Virtually amounts to use to use of any standard-sized cupboard, (j) stencil storing – cabinets for this purpose are found in libraries of two sized - 4 hangings each holding 50 offset plates or stencils and standard model with 14 hanging sections each storing 50 plates or a stencils (k) Transfer case - available in octavo, quarto fools cape or music (15" x 11 1/2") size are fitted with an interior spring clip. Besides these there are items of furniture in this section that have partially been included in the earlier sections. However, listing them - a) *suspension units* - A series of upright and bracket gives open access for lateral filling pockets, units can be wall fixed or free standing and are found in one to 4 tiers ; (b) *Stationery cabinets* – 3 to 10 drawers models for

quart or fools cape papers ; (c) punched card storage A wide range of dutch factory fabricated punched card trays, sorter racks and card cabinets are available ; (d) plan cabinets – Vertical plan cabinets, primarily for the filling of working drawings, with a capacity into 600 drawing which are suspended and can be divided with the help of visible guides ; (e) Microfilm storage – of various capacities (9 drawers, 3 compartments for 16 or 35 mm films) and (11 drawers double cabinets suitable for 5" × 3" microcards - capacity 47000 cards 7–9 drawer double cabinets 35 mm film (capacity up to 450 100' reels) (f) Gramophone record cabinets - of different dimension (full down front - interior holding 150 12" and 100 7" record width 27" depth 15" height 29") and their multipliers with increased capacitive are found in the audio-visual sections of some of the central university libraries ; (g) filing cabinets - already described in the funiture section.

7. OFFICE EQUIPMENT

For an efficient office functioning, the following items of equipment are required :

7.1 Duplicating machines : Offset litho spirit ; stencil and Dry process machines.

7.2 Photo copiers : In Indian university libraries there is a variety of photocopiers – imported as well as of indigenous makes a new calumnies have entered the trade with foreign allobar ration.

Therefore, the global variety of photocopiers has become accessible - both directly - thought liberal concessions for educational purposes for the import of information technology through foreign collaboration means.

7.3 Type-writers : Most popular are remington rand and Godrej Manual, electronic and computer all the three approaches are available with computer lesser printer is the boon.

7.4 Dictating machines 10 to 12 minutes have been introduced in a few university libraries in India.

7.5 Telephone services : (intercommunication and answering) almost all the university libraries there have university intercom facilities of their own independent intercom facilities for the enhancement of officeiency. The librarian can convey messages for work to employees located at different floors of the library

7.6 Letter opening and sealing machines.

7.7 Collating machines

7.8 Electric stapling matching.

7.9.1. Guillotines

7.9.2. Document Shredders.

8. COMPUTER TECHNOLOGY WITH LAN, WAN, INTERNT, ERNET, FACILITIES

To increase efficiency to reduce errors and to release the professional for few more productive duties, U. G. C. Of India have provide grants for the application of new information technology with which two types of revolutions on the computerization of individual university library and their mutual networking within the country through INPLIBNET plan of U. G. C. Another opening is through information network. The list of equipment being acquired or acquired so far can be related as under :

(a) Computer – PC mini PC/AT compatible with INTEL 8086 Microprocessor with 2/4 MB/ram 30/40 MB HDD 5-25 DUAL PDD

(b) Soft-ware (Communication software-Novell Advanced) Not ware-15/higher

For Library operatical management support and infh. services:

(c) Electroatat machine cover

(d) Video-Cameral Cameras

(e) Audio-systems – Record player ; tape recorder/player and CD player

(r) VCR/VCP

(g) CD ROM

(h) Net working : Connecting system ; potent 2 ; modern (Modulator and Demodulator) Ethernet system/Archnet system.

(i) User interface – windows 3.0 of GEM

(j) Operating System – MS DOS/UNIX

(k) Printer – Dot Matrix/Laser Printer

(l) Tele – communication accessories ; Software Satellite Dish Antenna

(m) Satellite Dish Antenna

(n) Telephone/fax/fascimile/telex

(o) Directlines/lease/lines/dial up modes

(p) Local area serves needs work station : Interface-cards connecting cables : Twisted wire, coaxial cable, Fibre optic cable etc.

3

Library Furniture

The physical plan NIMS of a library is incomplete without proper furniture, fittings and furnishings. The right type of furniture can add to the functional effectiveness of the library to a great extent. Much of the library furniture has been standardized; and within the standardized dimensions there is a lot of variety available. Still every librarian must have adequate knowledge about library furniture and equipment, so that he may get suitable items of furniture for his library. A librarian does get a chance to design and purchase new furniture, at one time or the other, whether he is shifting to a new building or is working in an old one.

Bad quality and inappropriate design of library furniture can ruin the efficacy of a library. "Efficiency of the library operation is dependent to a large extent upon such typical small details as the interior of a charging tray, the clear height in the knee space section of a charging desk or under library tables, or the design of the library chairs with regard to posture; to mention only a few among scores of details." The importance of well suited furniture and equipment for a library cannot be overemphasized.

Library furniture should be strong, sturdy, functionally adequate, aesthetically pleasing, and of good quality. Some of these qualities are discussed below.

DURABILITY

Library furniture should be durable. Most of the furniture cannot be replaced frequently. It is far wiser initially to purchase fewer pieces of better quality and to add items later than to compromise a limited budget by purchasing inferior products which will create unending maintenance and repair problems. Library furniture is subjected to continuous rough and careless handling. Only sturdy and good quality furniture can withstand such handling for any reasonable length of time.

The quest for durability has led many librarians to go in for steel furniture. Wooden book-racks have almost been replaced by steel racks and for good reasons. Steel racks are more lasting, are easy to clean and are not prone to white ants as wooden racks are. Even chairs, tables and other items of furniture are now being made of non-wood material like plastic, steel, pressed wood (plywood) etc. It is becoming increasingly difficult to get good quality, seasoned wood. Our vanishing forests are responsible for this shortage of quality wood. With the increase in population the demand for timber and quality wood for furniture has increased many fold. There are not enough trees let tin the country to meet that demand. It has become imperative to go in for substitutes like plastic, steel and other material for house building as well as furniture. Librarians have to reconcile to this development. Scarcity of wood has made wooden furniture more expensive than furniture made of steel, pressed wood and even plastic. There is certain dinity, certain elegance in furniture made of good quality wood like teak and rosewood. The absence of such elegant furniture will be felt throughout the world. But librarians cannot do anything in this matter and have to select and buy whatever is available in the market and most suited to the needs of the library.

FUNCTIONALISM

Furniture is not merely for decoration. It is kept because each piece serves a specific function. And each item must be judged by the efficacy with which it serves the function assigned to it. Therefore, it is important for the librarian to consider each item of furniture in relation to the job it is intended to perform. However strong and sturdy, however ornate and pleasing a piece of furniture may be, it loses all its value if it is functionally defective. Nobody would like to sit in a chair in which he will feel uncomfortable after fifteen minutes or use a table under which his knees would be painfully squeezed. It is irritating to use a catalogue, the drawers of which stick, and if pulled hard come out and fall down with a bang.

The implication is that the librarian must be very particular about the library. It is always advisable to go in for standard sizes, unless a librarian is convinced about the advantage of the variation he prefers. It would be better to get samples before accepting tenders so that the functional and other aspects of the furniture could be tested. It may not be quite easy for a librarian to judge the quality of wood and the durability of various joints but it should not be difficult to know whether a piece of furniture is functionally all right or not.

AESTHETIC APPEAL

In addition to the sturdiness and functional appropriateness, the library furniture should be pleasing to the eye, both in design and finish. It should be inviting and must add to the beauty and aesthetic appeal of the place where it is kept.' Too often, especially in libraries, qualities of design and style have been ignored and a drab, depressing appearance is the inevitable result. An atmosphere that is both inviting and harmonious should be sought after and this can be accomplished only by careful consideration to the architectural concept of the building and the relation of the individual pieces to each other."[21] Library as a cultural and intellectual expression of the community must be pleasing and attractive, unlike a classroom.

STANDARDIZATION

After many years of tests and trials, librarians have been able to set certain standard specifications for library furniture and equipment. There are many obvious advantages of having furniture of standard dimensions in a library. The risk of its proving uncomfortable, unfunctional or useless is avoided. Functional efficiency is secured without much effort on the part of an individual librarian. We must learn from the experience of our precursors, and even of contemporaries who have gone deeper into the subject.

Bureau of Indian Standards have done pioneering work in this country by bringing out "Specifications for library furniture and fittings" IS : 1869 Part I Timber (196[illegible]). It was revised in 1978. The second standard (IS: 1829) Part ii (1977) (Steel) covers steel furniture. These standards, however, are not very comprehensive and do not cover all items of furniture and equipment. Under the circumstances, a librarian is almost on his own in designing or selecting items of furniture available in the market.

Even the adoption of standardized furniture does not mean uniformity in design and monotony in look. The sectional committee of the BIS also endorses this view. They write: "In laying down the dimensions and other features of the furniture required for library, the Committee realised the need of prescribing the essential functional requirements of each item of furniture leaving enough scope for the designer to vary the actual shape, aesthetics etc." Other authors have also voiced the view that standardization should be adopted only where necessary. "While shelves and catalogue trays should be standard, tables and chairs need not be. Given durability, good workmanship, and a sufficient amount of space per reader, tables may be round, medium, long or short, topped with linoleum or hardwood according to fitness and space, and variously designed." But items like catalogue cabinet, circulation counter, book racks must be of standard size.

4

Important Items of Furniture

1. BOOK RACKS

One of the most important items of furniture in a library is the book rack. A librarian should be very careful in selecting book racks for his library because it is an expensive item and cannot be discarded very often.

Single or Double Faced ?

Both single faced and double faced racks are required in every library. Single faced racks are used against walls. All the wall space available must be used most economically but at the same time an illusion of spaciousness] should be maintained. Wall shelving has become very popular and every library, big or small, is vying with each other in having as much wail space for shelving as possible, even at the expense of windows. Wall shelving is not a bad thing, if properly planned and effectively used. But only a very small library can exclusively depend upon wall space for shelving books and periodicals. As libraries grow, more space is required for shelving and so on [stack arrangement is required. In the stack room, double faced racks are invariably used because they are economical and do not spread the storage space widely apart.

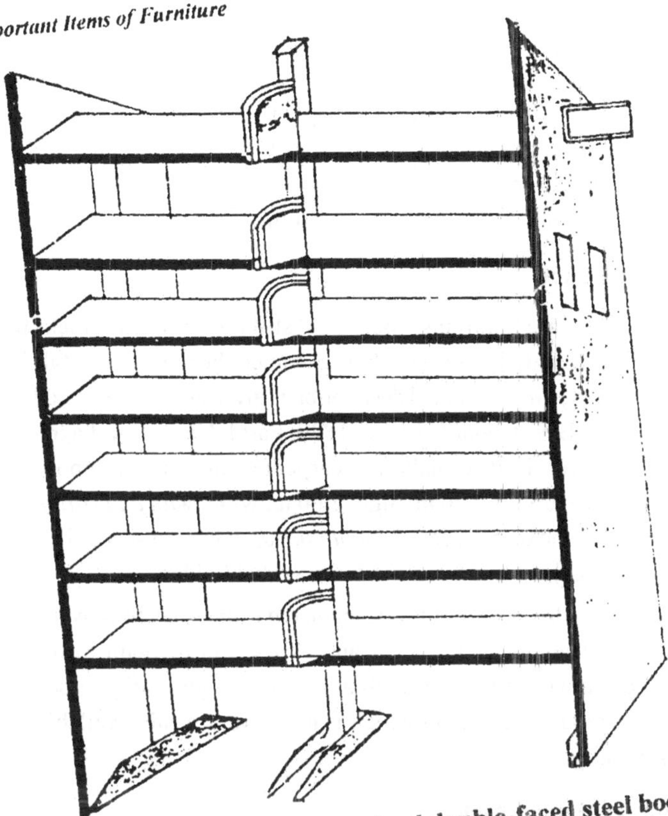

Plate 1. A conventional standard double-faced steel book-rack with seven shelves

Material

Another decision a librarian has to make about book racks is regarding its material: whether he should go in for steel racks or wooden racks. Today steel racks have almost completely replaced wooden racks for reasons already stated earlier. Steel racks are available in different sizes; the most common size preferred by librarians is 3 feet wide, 7.5 feet high and 0.75 feet deep. Double faced racks are naturally 1.5 feet deep. Racks with less height are also available.

A combination of wood and steel is increasingly being used for book racks, in many countries. Wooden panels fitted discreetly to steel frames lend elegance. These planks are usually detachable; meant to give support to the shelf and to brighten up the stacks. Such racks can be ordered in this country by giving design and specifications to a standard steel furniture manufacturer.

Wooden Rack

There are librarians who would still prefer wooden racks to steel ones mainly because of their elegance. For those who fall in this category, a most detailed description is given about a unit wooden rack by the BIS standard No. IS : 1829, Part I. Necessary diagrams are also given in it to make the carpenter understand important details. Each unit is 2.20 m. high, 2.00 m. wide *(with a partition in the middle)* and 0.45 m. deep *(double sided).* It has got seven shelves which are adjustable. Each shelf has a label holder.

Two observations may be made regarding such huge wooden racks. 1. They are very heavy and as a result difficult to move without extra hired hands in a library. 2. Very high quality seasoned wood is required for them which is not always easily available in this country.

Counter Height Racks

However, wooden racks can be used with advantage when the height of the racks has to be much smaller than the full height of 7.5 feet. Counter height racks can be used underneath windows and around the reading areas. In the latter case, they serve as partition without obstructing the view for vigilance and without slicing the openness and spaciousness of the reading areas. These smaller racks are better suited for shelving heavy reference sets which make it convenient for readers to use them. Even when made of teak wood, they are not very heavy because of their smaller size. Apart from the utilization of such space which otherwise would have been wasted. counter height racks break the monotony which standard sized racks inevitably create and add a touch of elegance which always goes with fine grained and well polished wood.

Plate 2. A non-conventional light steel book-rack with five shelves

Counter height racks are usually 40 inches high having three or four shelves according to the size of books to be shelved. The width and depth should be the same as that of a standard sized rack, unless there is need for deeper shelves.

Adjustability

Much has been written on the desirability of adjustable shelves. A book rack should have adjustable shelves because the size of books differ and oversized books may have to be accommodated by moving the shelves up or down by a few inches. In theory it all sounds wonderful and convenient but in actual practice adjustability of shelves is seldom put into use. To adjust and readjust shelves involves lot of work - taking down all the books from the affected shelves, adjusting the shelves in new positions and reshelving the books. Many shelves may have to be moved up or down to readjust one shelf. Few librarians actually have time and patience to do this much work for adjusting shelves, especially when the position of books on the shelves is never permanent. It is better to create an oversized and undersized hook sequences and to have racks with almost fixed shelves. The racks meant for oversized and undersized sequences will have shelves adjusted according to the sizes of books which have to be shelved on them.

A New Trend

A new trend in the design of library racks has emerged. Very simple, light but sturdy and functional book racks have been introduced, and more and more libraries are going in for such racks including British and American libraries. A British librarian observes, "So, increasingly, the librarians have looked abroad for furniture which fits their new vision of the library. While our (British) librarians, architects and designers suffered from the effects of financial restrictions the Scandinavians and the West Germans have taken advantage of their more favourable opportunities to develop purpose designed furniture of high quality ... This furniture is characterised by its lightness, simplicity and a style which emphasizes function. It makes attractive use of combinations of wood and metal and frequently takes a unit form which offers scope for flexibility and variety of arrangement."

The German librarians also have taken greater liberties with

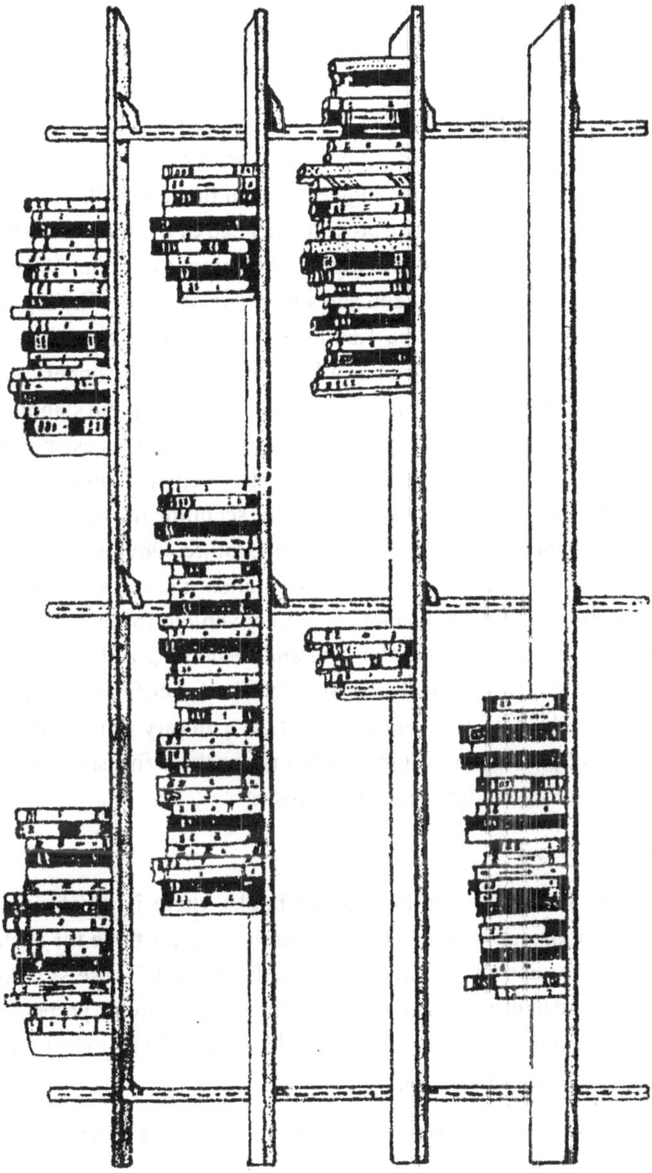

Plate 3. A non-conventional wall-hanging type book-rack

standardized racks. While they have stuck to the unit width of one meter or three feet, the height of book racks have been varied to suit the convenience of readers. "Modern practice is to mount the book cases so that the reader need not bend down to reach the bottom shelf and need not struggle to reach the top shelf. For this reason, only five shelves are provided instead of the former seven. The bottom shelf should have a ground clearance of about 50 cm; with a shelf spacing of 27 cm. and a thickness of 2 cm. The top of the uppermost shelf will be 1.68 m. Leigh." It must be admitted that 7.5 feet height for a rack is a little too much. The uppermost shelf cannot be reached by the majority of readers without standing on a stool. Even the sixth shelf is not conveniently accessible to many. Also, the lowermost shelf is very inconvenient to use : either the reader has to sit down on the floor for scanning the books on it or he has to bend- not a very convenient posture. Obviously, these racks will not be as economical as the standard seven shelf racks but they will decidedly be much more convenient for the readers. Moreover, on these racks, shelving and reshelving of books will be done more expeditiously. So also the shelf rectification work. Smaller racks also look more elegant. If a library is not facing acute space problem, it would be better to use these five shelf racks rather than the standard seven shelf ones.

Book-Supports

As shelves are seldom full of books, there is an obvious need for book-supports in adequate number - almost one for each shelf. Book-supports are invariably made of steel. These should be sturdy and high enough to support even the large volumes properly. Several manufacturers dealing in steel furniture like Godrej and Pilco manufacture book-supports.

2. PERIODICAL DISPLAY AND STORAGE RACKS

Three types of periodical racks are required in a library :

1. For displaying current issues;

2. For storing recent unbound issues; and
3. For shelving bound volumes.

Display Racks

For displaying loose issue of periodicals, special type of racks are used. They are of several designs.

Full Height Rack with Slanting Shelves

In this type of display racks shelves are either fixed or move on hinges. The movable variety has the advantage of providing space for storing the loose, back issues behind the shelves. Another advantage is that the whole periodical is visible while on display. *(see diagram)* This type of rack is usually single-faced so that it may be used against a wall. But two unit racks can be used back to back, if desired, to serve as a double faced rack. The dimensions commonly used are: 66 inches high, 48 inches wide and 22 inches deep and it has five shelves. It will accommodate about 35 periodicals.

The other commonly used type is the built-in stair type, *(see diagram)* It is 3 to 4 feet wide. There are built-in 'stairs' on which periodicals stand. While on display, only the upper portions of periodicals are visible. Elastic spring wires are used to keep periodicals erect.

One disadvantage of this type of rack is that periodicals which are smaller in size get sunk and are often not visible and the larger ones often bend over. To overcome this defect wooden blocks can be placed underneath smaller sized periodicals. These blocks should be of different thickness to suit various sizes of periodicals.

Other Display Methods

If partitioned reading tables are used in the periodical room, the partition can be used for displaying periodicals on both the sides by simply fixing flexible spring wire to it with the help of two hooks.

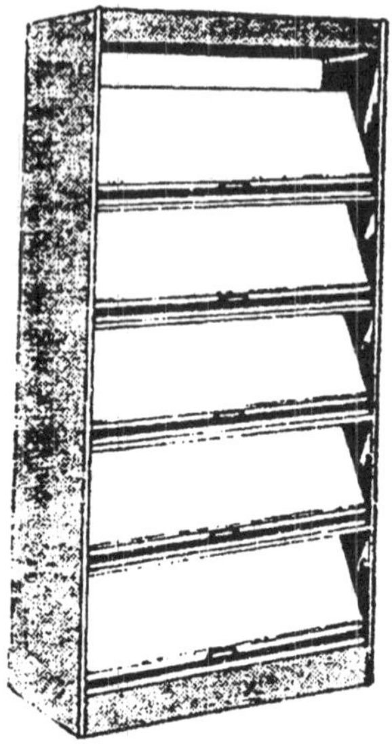

Plate 4. Wooden periodical display rack. Back loose issues are stored behind the movable shelves

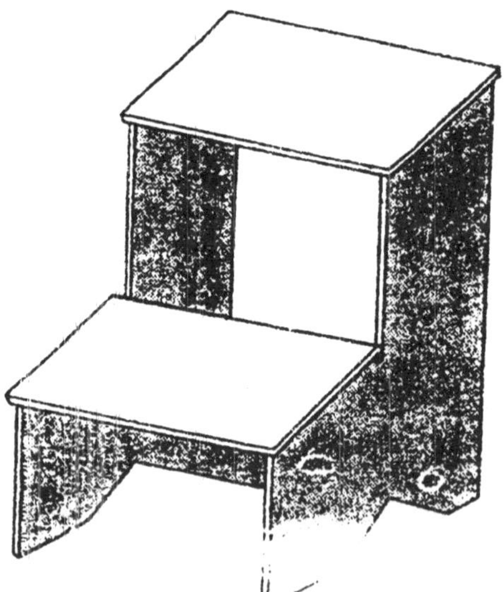

Plate 5. A wooden step-stool

Plate 6. A round steel stood on wheels

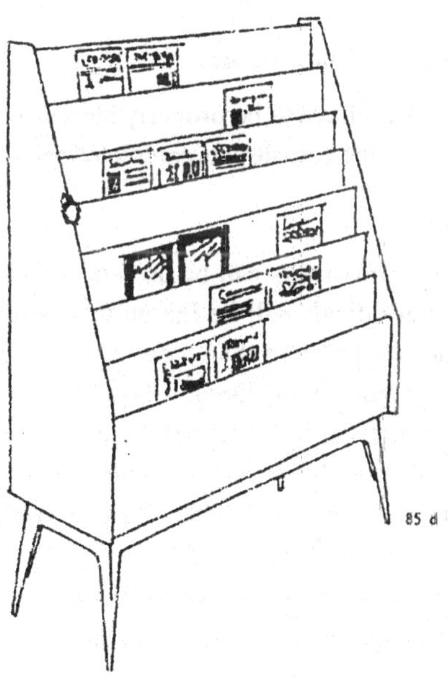

Plate 7. Stair-type wooden periodical display rack

If the number of periodicals subscribed by a library is quite large, it may not be possible to display all the subscribed periodicals. Some of the less used ones may have to be sent directly to the storage shelves meant for loose numbers.

Some libraries use ordinary book-racks for displaying current issues of periodicals when the number of periodicals subscribed is large. This is being done in Research Library of Banaras Hindu University.

Is Display Necessary ?

Some librarians find it very cumbersome to display current numbers of periodicals, and have dispensed with display racks altogether thus saving valuable space for other purposes. But there is no denying of the tact that displaying of periodicals does help the reader to know the new arrivals at a glance which he may miss otherwise. Colourful magazines also lend brightness to the periodical room and help in attracting readers.

Storage Racks for Loose Issues

Loose issues have to be properly stored so that they can be retrieved easily till the volume gets completed and is sent for binding.

Ordinary Racks

Ordinary book racks can be used economically for storing loose issues. Periodicals will lie flat on the shelves. The depth of the shelves should be more than what is required for book racks and the height should be considerably less. The suitable dimensions are: height 5.5 feet, depth 1.5 feet and breadth 4.5 feet. The space between shelves may be six to seven inches instead of the usual nine inches, so that seven to eight shelves can be easily accommodated inspite of the lesser height.

As in the case of books, single faced racks can be used against walls and double faced can be most economically arranged in stack formation.

Avoid Rigidity

Racks having pigeon holes should be avoided as they are too rigid and are wasteful of space. Another type is that of cupboards having drawers. The same element of rigidity is in this type also. If the periodical is of small size, there will be wastage of space and if too large, it will not go in and has to be shelved separately unless the pigeon holes or the drawers are made extraordinarily large. But the larger the pigeon holes, the greater will be the wastage of space.

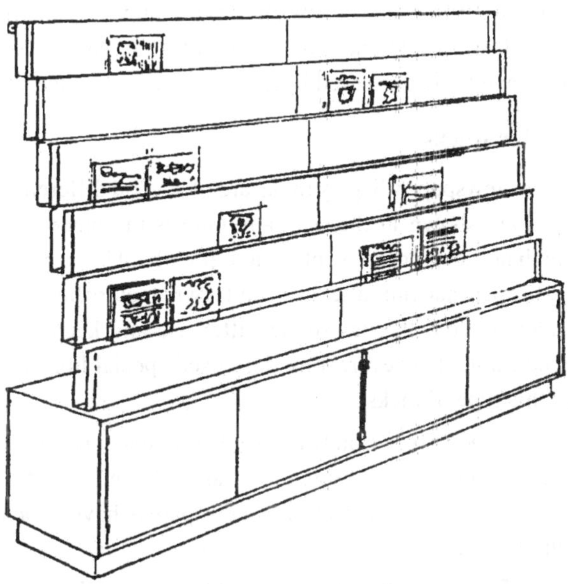

Plate 8. Another type of wooden periodical display rack. Loose issues are stored in the cupboards underneath

Whatever type of racks is used, it must have movable label-holders with names of periodicals written on them so that periodicals may come back at the proper places easily after consultation. Label-holders are much more important for periodical racks having loose issues than even for book racks.

Bound Volumes

For storage of bound volumes of periodicals, ordinary book racks are used. An average periodical is larger than an ordinary book therefore racks meant for storing bound volumes of periodicals may have one shelf less than the book racks so that bound volumes could be shelved easily.

3. NEWSPAPER RACKS

Displaying and storing of newspapers have always been a problem for librarians. Newspapers are unwieldy in size and thus difficult to handle and store. They also get easily torn. But still they have to be preserved because of their reference value.

Display Racks

Newspaper display racks are of several different types. Two types arc shown in the diagram. One is the pigeon-hole type in which newspapers are kept folded. It will not be easy to restore the newspaper each time after use. And it will require highly responsible readers to fold the newspaper after use and keep it back in the pigeon-hole. However, some less used special libraries can go in for this type of racks.

Another type is in which each newspaper is kept in a wooden rod. And the rods are hung on a frame. A couple of frame-design are shown in the diagrams. The newspapers have to be read along with the rod.

The simplest method would be to keep the newspaper flat on the reading tables and leave them to their fate.

Storage

Newspapers are best stored on microfilms. But to read microfilms, a microfilm-reader is necessary. And every library does not possess a microfilm-reader, even if it succeeds in procuring microfilms. The other obvious alternative is to get the newspaper bound and shelve them flat on suitable racks. It is common experience in many libraries that newspapers, at the end of a day, are torn to pieces by readers and are not in a proper condition to be sent for binding. Some libraries subscribe to extra copies of newspapers which are directly sent for binding. Every library may not be able to afford these extra copies.

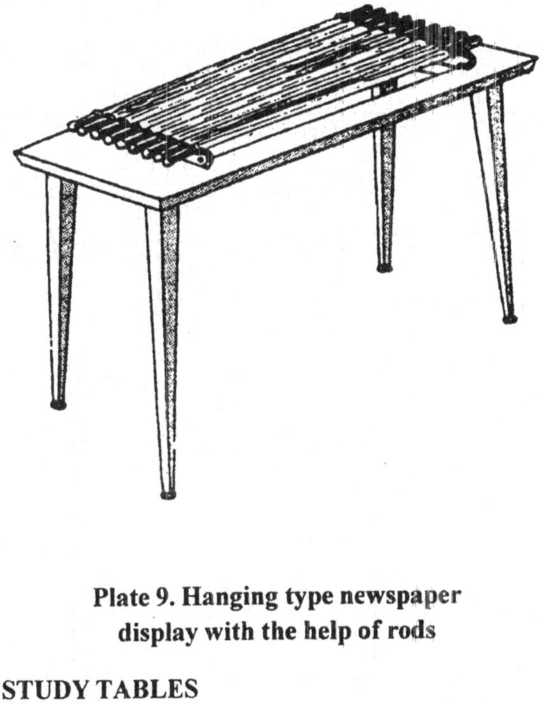

Plate 9. Hanging type newspaper display with the help of rods

4. STUDY TABLES

Study tables in the reading room need not adhere to uniformity in size and design. To break the monotony and drabness and to create a pleasing effect in a reading room, it is essential to have a variety of reading tables. But all reading tables must adhere to standard sizes.

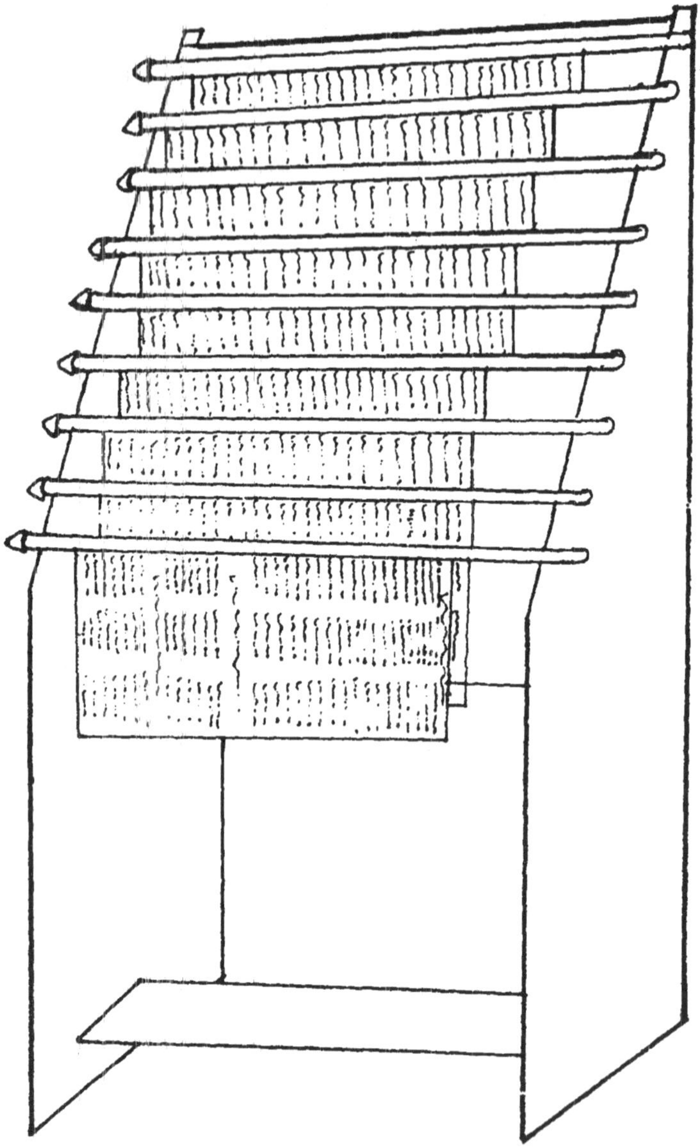

Plate 10. Another design for hanging type newspaper display rack

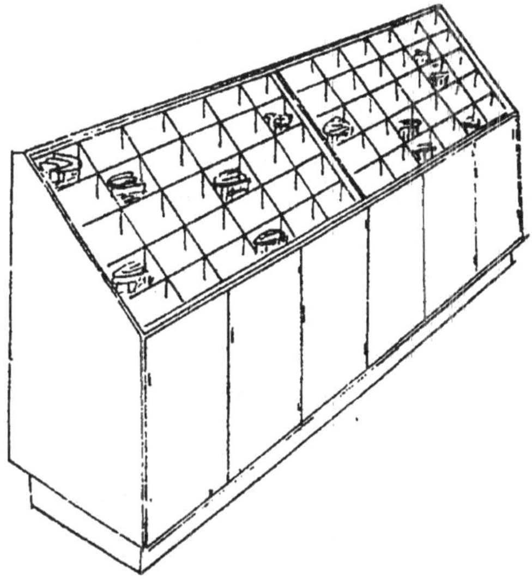

Plate 11. Pigeon-hole type newspaper display rack

ISI Recommendation

Single Faced

The standard size recommended by BIS is 2m x 7m (6'.6" X 2'.3").(33) It is presumably meant for three readers. From the dimensions it is clear that readers have to sit only on one side of the table. In other words, all the readers will be facing the same side and not each other. This will avoid distraction and disturbance to serious readers, *(see diagram)*

Other Standard Sizes

The other usual sizes for single sided tables are :

60 X 100 cm. (2' X 3.25') For one reader

60 X 170 cm. (2' X 5.9') For two readers

60 X 240 cm. (2' X 8') For four readers

Single sided reading tables seem to be quite popular in Russian libraries.

Single faced tables, however, give a look of monotony and regimentation and also occupy more space per reader. Both single and double faced tables may be used in a room to avoid regimentation — even in Russia.

Double Faced

The standard sizes for double faced tables are :

1m X 1m (3' X 3.5')	For two readers (facing each other)
1m X 1.5m (3' X 5')	For four readers
1m X 2.25m (3'X 7'.6")	For six readers
1m X 3m (3' X 10')	For eight readers

Tables for more than eight readers should be avoided in a library. They become too heavy and unwieldy to move.

Round Tables

Round tables are still popular in many libraries. "It is generally advisable to include one to four round tables, depending on the size, proportions and arrangement of the room. Round tables help to relieve angularity of appearance. Often one round table is sufficient except in very large rooms; more than two will be superfluous. A room that is completely filled with round tables is as monotonous as one that contains nothing but rectangular tables."(1)

It may be said against the round table that it is not very convenient for the reader to work for long hours because he has to use convex periphery. There is also waste of space if round tables are used singly. But round tables do add to the beauty of the reading rooms and must be tolerated.

Height

The standard height of reading tables is 0.75m. or 30 inches. Some readers prefer 28" height - especially those who are short

Study Tables

Single Faced

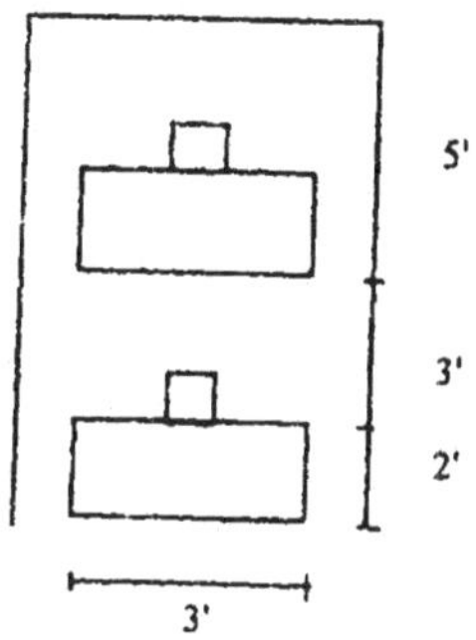

Single Seater

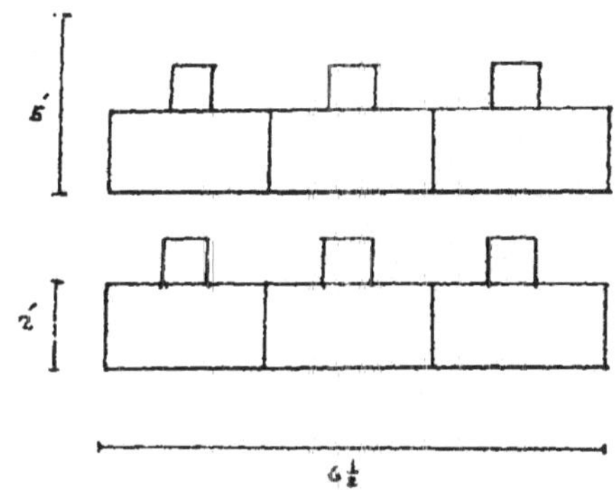

Three seater single faced as recommended by the Bureau of Indian Standards

Double Faced

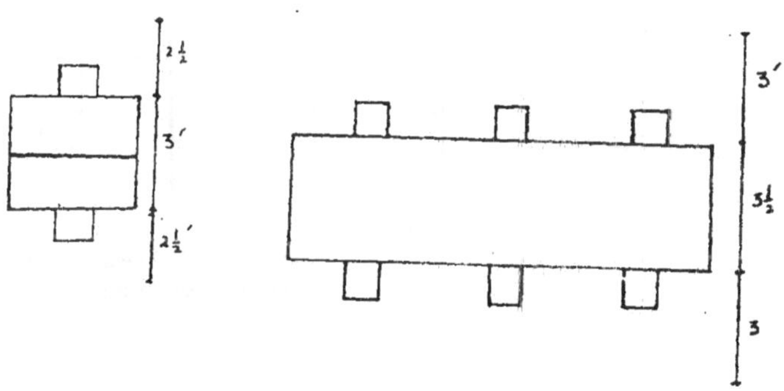

Plate 12.

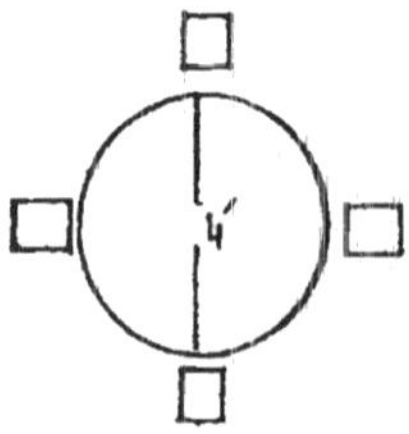

Round table

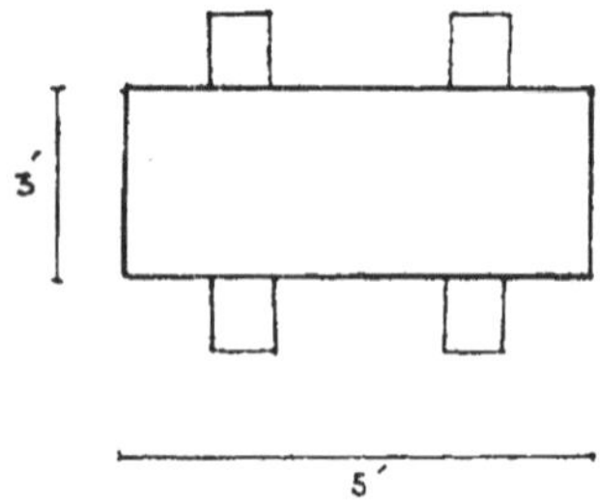

Double faced four seater table

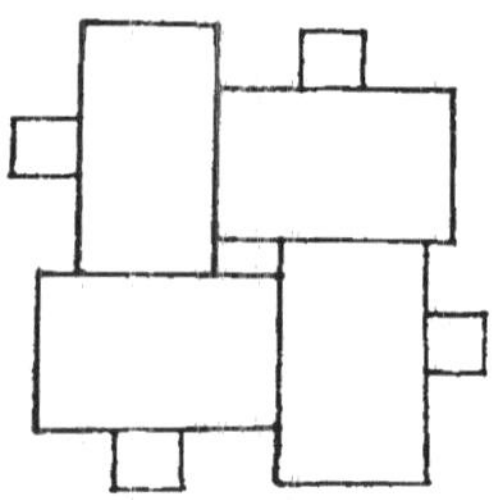

Single Seater tables in cyclic formation.

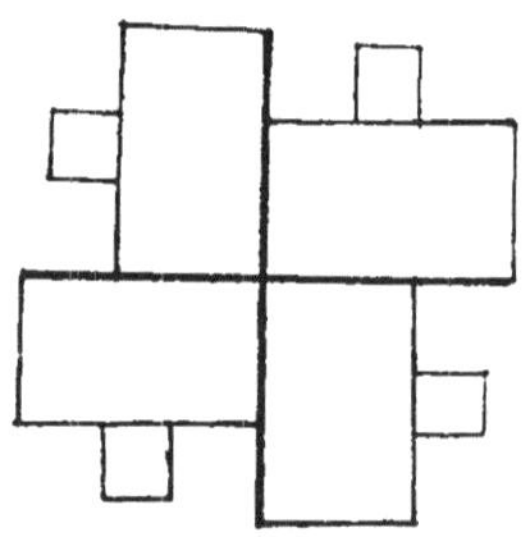

Another type of arrangement of cyclic formation of single seater tables.

Plate 13

statured. In children section of public libraries, the height of tables naturally will be much less.

The diameter of a round reading table to seat four readers should be four feet.

Other Shapes

Single faced tables arranged in cyclic formation *(see diagram)* are increasingly used in academic and research libraries. This arrangement offers privacy to a reader without occupying additional space. If partitions are used on the tables this formation almost serves as cubicles.

Office tables come in standard sizes usually with drawers. These will be required in the various work rooms in the library. Most of the office tables have steel frames with wooden, laminated top.

Other Considerations

The legs of a reading table should be well under the table so that proper knee space is provided for all the readers uniformly. There is nothing more irritating than a table which constantly hits your knees. There should also be proper foot rests provided. The tops of reading tables should be covered with laminated plastic to protect them from scratches, chinks and cracks.

Placing of Reading Tables

The placing and arrangement of reading tables in reading rooms should be considered at the time of planning a new building and details be worked out before actual construction starts. In fact, the placing of tables and chairs should be shown in the plan itself or in a separate drawing.

The foremost consideration in the arrangement of tables has to be the utilisation of natural light. The tables should be arranged in a way that adequate light falls from the windows on the tables but at the same time glare is avoided. It would mean that readers should not sit facing the windows. Windows should be on their sides. If the reading room is of proper dimensions and the windows are tall enough, all the reading tables will have adequate natural light. Only on very cloudy days there may be need to switch on the electric light during the day time.

The gangway between two tables should be six feet, if double faced and four feet, if single faced. This will provide enough space for the chairs and for the flow of traffic. The aisles between the ends of tables should be four feet wide. The central aisle should be six feet wide.

5. CHAIRS

Chairs in the reading room should be comfortable, sturdy and elegant in design. Comfort is perhaps the most essential factor. The dimensions and design of reading room chairs should be such that the reader may not feel uncomfortable after a short period. His legs should not hang in the air but should touch the ground while sitting erect. When he is reclining, his legs should be able to rest on the bar at the lower part of the table meant for the purpose. There is a consensus of opinion that the seat of the chair should be 18 inches high measured from the floor. .

The design of the chair should allow the weight of the body of the occupant to be as much on the bottom as possible: the thighs should not share much weight. To make this possible the back portion of the seat of the chair should be about one inch lower than the front portion. If, however, the seat is made of flexible material like cane, the seat automatically achieves this.

The back rest of the chair should be slightly curved to give maximum comfort to the back of the reader. It is found that the curved support gives more comfort to the back than a flat one.

Chairs which are meant for reading should have full or half arms so that a reader may be able to rest his arms while reading in a reclined position. Chairs meant for writing need not have any arms. It would mean that, in a reading room, there should be chairs with as well as without arms and readers should be allowed to make their choice. The design of the chair be such that it is easy to get into and get out of it, even for a rather bulky person.

Chairs in work-room should preferably be armed; and at the issue counter wheeled chair would be convenient to move around *(see diagrams)*

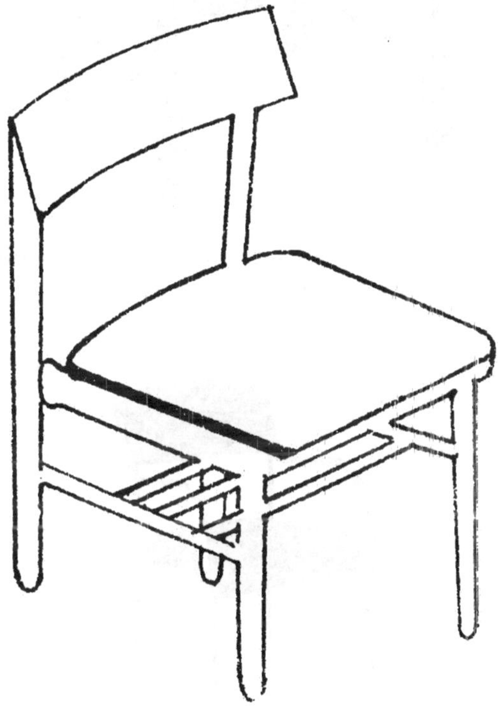

Plate 14. Wooden armless chair with wooden seat and curved back

Plate 15. Wooden chair with cushioned seat in classic style having short arms

Plate 16. Steel armed chair with cushioned seat

Plate 17. Steel armless chair on wheels for circulation counter work

People vary in height and girth. The same chair may not be comfortable for different sizes of people. It will be ideal to have chairs suited to different sizes of people; but may not be quite a practical proposition.

Cushioned chairs for the reading room should be avoided in a tropical country like India. Padded and upholstered seats become sticky in summer and rainy seasons. If of cheap quality, cushioned chairs are not as durable as wooden or even caned chairs. Wooden seats on the other hand are rather hard and are not suitable for long sittings. Caned seats can be quite lasting and comfortable, if properly made. To make a caned seat more lasting, a frame two inches wide on all sides, should be fitted in the seat of the chair and the cane should be woven in the frame and not in the outer-structure. In this way, only the middle of the seat is cane-woven and the peripheries are of wood. This gives extra strength to the seat. The cane should be woven like a mat and not like a mesh.

To reduce noise, the lower tips of the legs should have rubber pads.

BIS Recommendation

The recommendations of the BIS for the library chair are as follows :

(a) The height of the seat shall be 45 cm. from the floor level.

(b) The average width of seat measured midway across the width and depth of seat shall be 43 cm., the seat being wider at the front by 5 cm.

(c) The arms shall be 200 mm. high from the seat and set back 75 mm. from the front edge of seat.

(d) The back rest shall be curved in plan and shall be not more than 180 mm. in height measured from the arm rest.(3)

6. CIRCULATION COUNTER

Issue counter is an expensive item of furniture and cannot be replaced very often. Therefore much thought and calculation should go into estimating requirements for charging, discharging of books and into deciding upon the size and design of the counter.

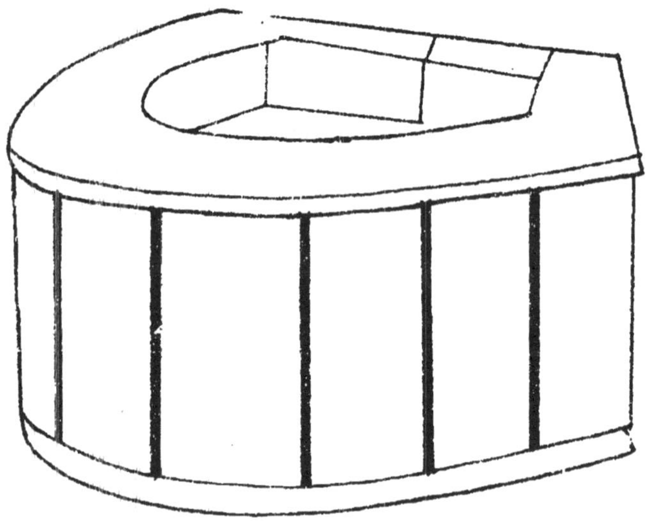

Plate 18. Semi-circular circulation counter for smaller libraries

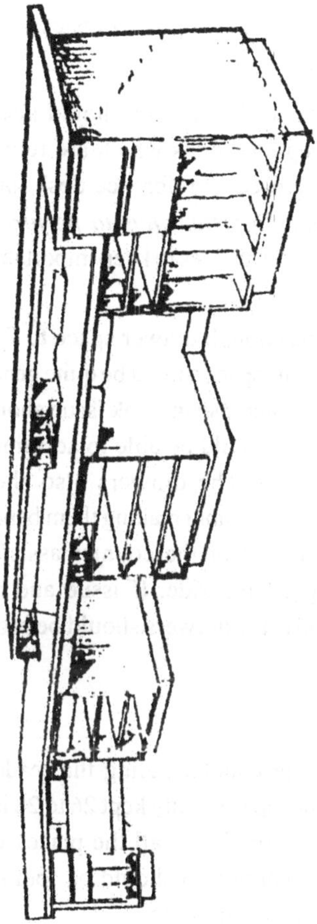

Plate 19. Sized circulation counter

Issue counter has to perform the following functions:

1. Registeration of new readers.
2. Charging or issue of books.
3. Discharging or receiving books back.
4. Reservation of books lent out.

Obviously enough the counter should also have adequate shelving space to keep the books which are returned. And if the counter has also to be used as reference desk *(in small libraries where the same library assistant has to perform both the jobs)* there should be a few extra shelves to keep important ready reference books.

There should be enough drawer space to file book cards of all the books lent out. This space should be quite generously provided and the possible future increase in book issue should be taken into account. These drawers should be able to accommodate the book cards used in the library The drawers also should be able to accommodate guide cards without making them bend. These drawers should be as near the seat of the counter assistant as possible, preferably on his right hand side. If issue and return are to be administered separately, the drawers should be provided near both the seats.

Dimensions

The height of the counter facing the reader should be 40 inches. The width at the top is usually kept 26 to 28 inches. Adequate knee space should be provided at all the places where assistants have to sit and work. There also should be foot rest to make the sitting comfortable for longer hours.

Design

It is difficult to suggest the exact length and design of the counter which may suit every library. There are various designs in vogue : rectangular; L shaped; U shaped; circular etc. Whatever design is selected, it is better to have the counter in small units of 3 feet each. The units may be bolted together or just placed adjacent to each other to give the illusion of one piece. The unit type counter is easy to shift from one place to another and also can be extended whenever need arises.

A slick, elegant and functional counter should be preferred to a huge monolithic monster. Avoid having railings at the top which serve literally as a screen between the readers and the staff. Railings or glass screen create cold formality, become dirty, and prove a hindrance to easy conversation in low tones. Easy exchange of books also is not possible.

The top should be either of hard well-polished wood or should be covered with linolium or laminated plastic.

If circulation is automated by the use of computers there will hardly be need to keep records manually as in Brown or Newark systems. The circulation counter, in that case, will be much simpler and sleek. There are firms which specialize in making furniture specially for computer operators. These are simple, elegant and innovative in design. Some of these firms are listed in the Appendix.

7. CATALOGUE CABINET

Catalogue cabinet is quite a complicated piece of furniture and must be made by ail exporenced carpenter out of highly seasoned wood. Ready made cabinets are also available with dealers of library equipment and furniture. *(See Appendix for list of dealers)*

Care should be taken to ensure that:

1. The dimensions, especially of the inner side of the drawers, are accurate. The drawer should not jam and should come out and go in with ease.
2. The whole structure, including the drawers, should be sturdy and made of hard wood like teak. The wood used should be highly seasoned so that drawers do not get stuck during the rainy season.

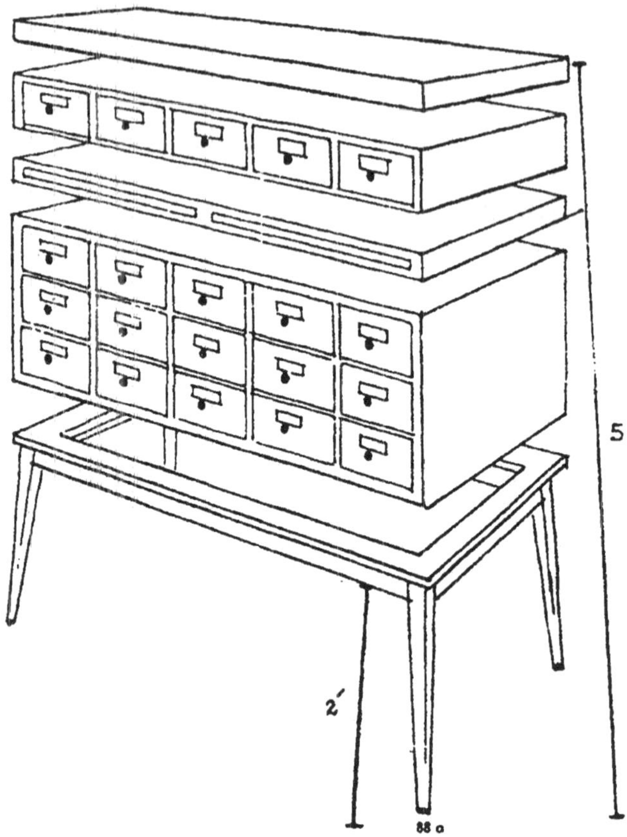

Plate 20. Catalogue Cabinet with 20 drawers showing the height of the stand and the uppermost part

It is better to have a modular cabinet rather than a big single-piece structure having hundreds of drawers. The standard recommended by the BIS is of 24 drawers. It could easily be of 30 or 20 drawers. Whatever size is selected, all the units should have the same number of drawers.

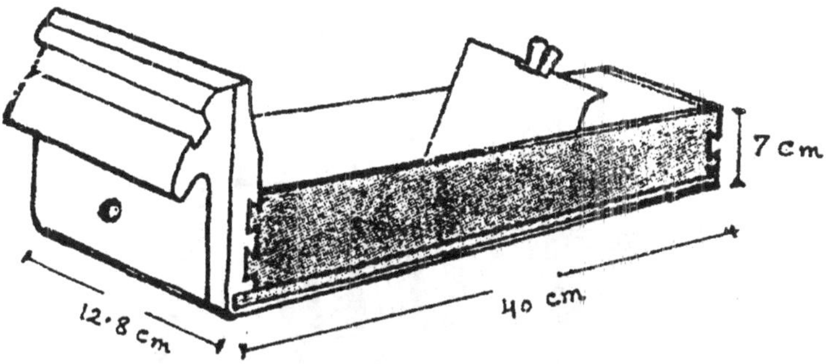

Plate 21. Details of a catalogue drawer

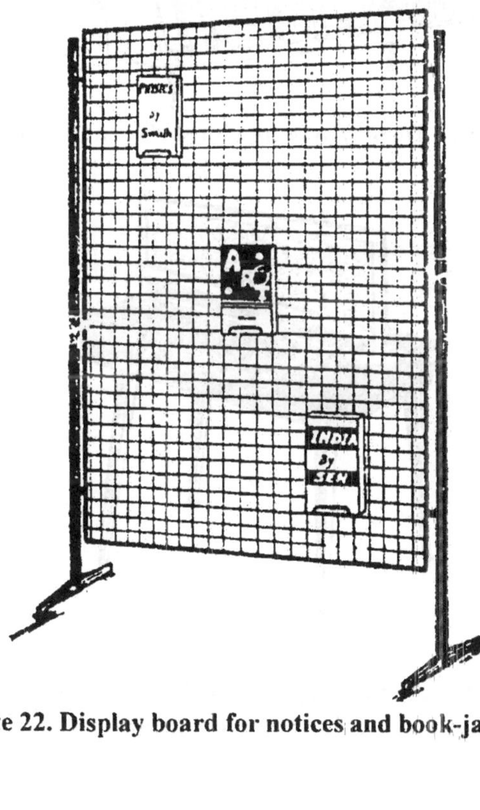

Plate 22. Display board for notices and book-jackets

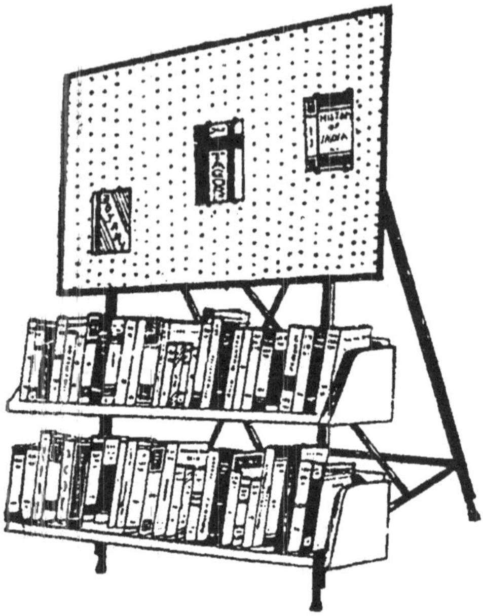

Plate 23. Display system with shelves and a board

Plate 24. Small display board with troughs for keeping books on display

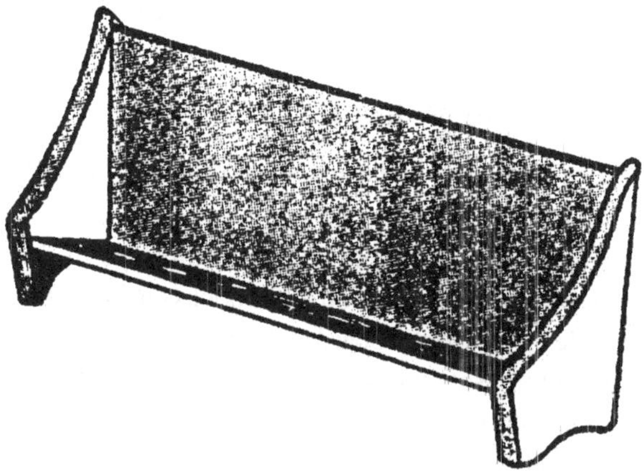

Plate 25. Single book trough to display a few books

Dimensions

The stand should be 24 inches high from the ground and the height of the cabinet should not exceed 5 feet from the ground. This can accommodate six trays vertically and five trays horizontally.

The recommended size of each tray is 12.8X7 cm. to hold 12.5X7.5 cm. catalogue cards. The inner breadth of the tray has to be a little more than of the card to allow easy movement of the cards and the inner height a little less so as to project the cards up for easy consultation. The length of the tray is usually 40 cm. or 16 inches. Each tray can hold about 1,000 cards of medium thickness. Each tray should have :

(a) A rod to hold the cards in position;

(b) Handle for pulling out trays conveniently;

(c) A label holder;

(d) Gravity action tray-catch to prevent the drawer from falling out;

(e) A wooden angle block inside the tray to keep the cards upright. *(see diagram)*

Steel catalogue cabinets should be avoided. They are noisy, dull looking and do not move smoothly.

8. BOOK DISPLAY RACK

Every library should have a few display racks. Three types are in common use :

1. One is display rack-cum-bulletin-board type. It is double faced having a display trough for books on either side and a double faced bulletin board at the centre. The bulletin board should have soft surface on which drawing pins or similar fixing material may easily be fixed. The book troughs on either side should be slightly slanting so that the spines of books on display could easily be read. The height of the book troughs should be about 3 feet from the floor. *(see diagram)* There can be more than one shelf on either side, *(see diagram)*

Plate 26. Encyclopedia stand

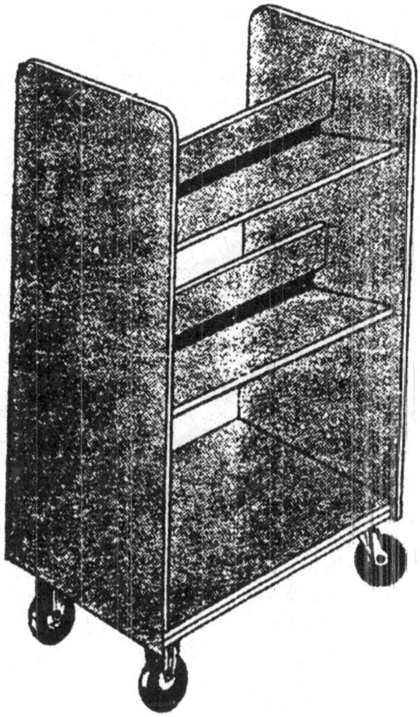

Plate 27. A Conventional type wooden trolley

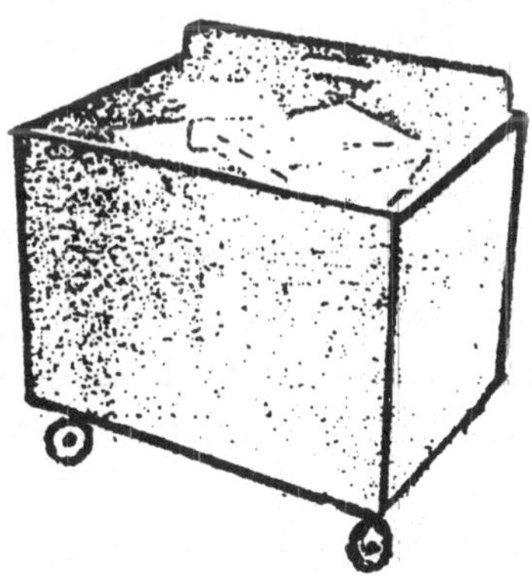

Plate 28. A box-like depressible type book trolley

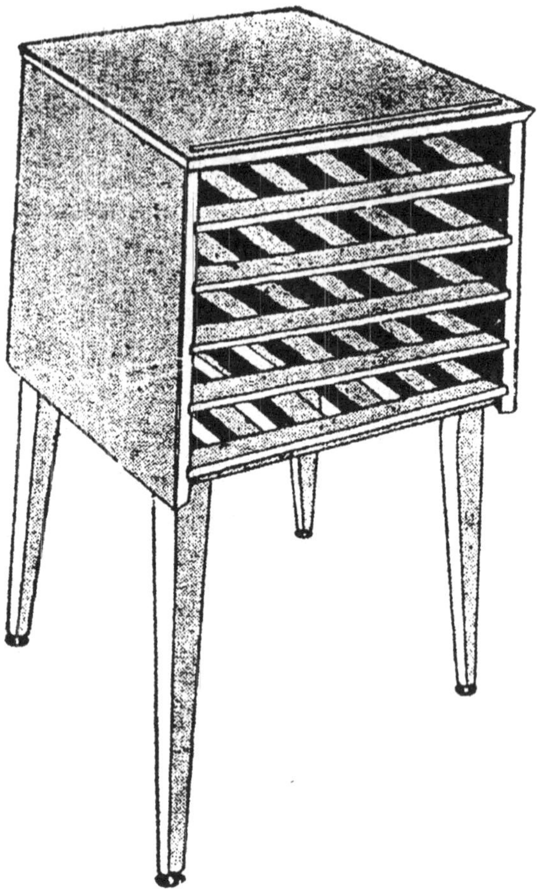

Plate 29. Atlas Stand

2. A smaller structure having only display troughs for books.
3. Portable single faced book trough to be kept on a table. It is used when a small, number of books have to be displayed. *(see diagram)*
4. A movable double shelf with a much bigger display board *(see diagram)*

9. DICTIONARY OR ENCYCLOPEDIA STAND

It is good to keep fat volumes of a multi-volumed dictionary or encyclopedia in a separate small rack. They add to the beauty of the area and it is convenient to handle books from a low height. Usually such racks have only two shelves with a sloping top. The width is generally matching the number of volumes to be accommodated. It is better to have some extra space in case the revised edition is expanded, *(see diagram)* These have to be in addition to counter height racks described earlier.

10. BOOK TROLLEY OR TRUCK

Every day books have to be transported from the issue counter to the stacks; from the acquisition section to the technical section; from the technical section to the stack room and occasionally have to be sent for binding and for arranging displays etc. It is convenient and economical to carry books from one place to another in a trolley rather than carry them manually. In a very small library the need of a trolley may not arise, but bigger libraries must have trolleys to carry books, *(see diagram)*

Another type of book trolley which is very much in use in American libraries is the Depressible Book Trolley. This self-levelling book-trolley is just a box 30" square and about two feet deep moving on four small wheels. There is a wooden plank inside the box which is movable and is fitted at the centre on a coil spring below. The plank is gradually depressed with the weight of the books. It can hold about 200 books of average size. The plank comes up automatically with the action of the coil spring when the books are removed. The coil spring, obviously, has to be very strong to go up and down with the load of books. It should be made of either steel or copper - non rusting metals.

11. ATLAS STAND

Atlases are often over sized pieces of documents and are

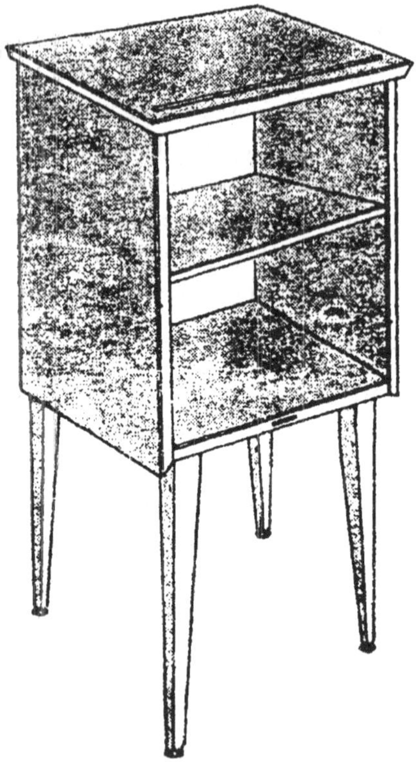

Plate 30. A smaller dictionary or encyclopedia stand with sloping top for consultation

very unwidely to handle and inconvenient to shelve on ordinary racks. It is better to keep them in a separate stand especially made for them, keeping in view the immense size of atlases. The height can be according to the requirements ranging from 3 to 5 feet, depth 2.5 feet and width 2 feet. The space between shelves should be about 4 inches. The top should be sloping which may be used for consulting atlases. *(see diagram)*

12. CARPETS AND FLOOR COVERS

Carpets give a pleasing look to the reading areas. They also reduce noise produced by walking feet and dragged chairs. Carpets in a library should not only be pleasing but also durable. Ordinary cotton carpets can be purchased in various sizes or can be made to order. These are cheap and easy to clean, but are not very durable. They also crinkle easily. Jute matting is available in very attractive designs and wears well. But its colours fade quickly and it is not very convenient to clean. It also gets pulled up and has the habit of developing permanent wrinkles. Therefore, it must be laid by experienced hands preferably from wall to wall. Wooden strips should be used to fix the position of edges near the walls to hold the carpet in proper position.

The best floor covering is perhaps rubber matting. It is lasting, smooth and can be cleaned easily. It is not very attractive and, of course, is expensive. But in the long run, it may prove cheaper. Laminated floor covering like linoleum comes in attractive shades. It is not very expensive and can be easily laid. It is often seen in computer rooms and offices throughout the country. Libraries can profitably use it. It does not crinkle and lasts for reasonably long periods.

Other Items of Furniture

Every library needs many more small but, nevertheless, important items of furniture, the details of which need not be given here. Some of these essential items are : Stools *(see diagram)* umbrella stands, map stands, waste paper baskets *(which should be available in abundance in all the areas).* Adequate number of stools should be available in the stack area. Movable stools on wheel are now available which will be convenient to use *(see diagram).*

APPENDIX

FURNITURE AND LIBRARY SUPPLIERS

1.	Alkosign Display Systems 70, C. Government Industrial Estate Kandivli (W) Bombay 400 067	Display racks
2.	American Library House 7/54 Punjabi Bagh (West) New Delhi	Library furniture and stationery items
3.	Appollo Furnishers B-62/10 Phase-II Naraina Industrial Area New Delhi 110028	Steel furniture including racks
4.	Charan Metal Corporation H.O. 101 A, Udyog Nagar Kanpur U.P.	-do-
5.	Donewell Rotaries R 694 (First Floor) New Rajender Nagar New Delhi 110060	Stool (Rolling)
6.	Equipments International Rang Vaibhav Khandke Building 9, R.K.Vaidya Road Dadar Bombay 400 028	Mobile rack systems
7.	Eurotech Design Systems P. Ltd. Veer Savarkar Marg Shivaji Park Bombay 400 028	For specially designed chairs
8.	Godrej & Boyce Mfg. Co. Ltd. Pirojshah Nagar Vikhroli Bombay 400 079	For steel furniture and rucks

9.	Hi-Tech Modular Systems (India) Pvt. Ltd. D-28/1, MIDC Industrial Area T.T.C. Turbhe (Near Turbhe Tele Exchange) New Bombay 400613	Cubicles and computer furniture including chairs
10.	I.G. Enterprises 452-C/33, Onkar Nagar - C Tri Nagar Delhi 110035	
11.	India Linoleum Birla Building 9/1, R.N. Mukherjee Road Calcutta 700 001	Flooring material
12.	Kirloskar Electrodyne Ltd. 117, 'S' Block, MIDC Bhosari, Pune 411 026	Modular furniture for computers
13.	Library Emporium 124 A/187, Govind Nagar Kanpur 208 006	
14.	Maruti Steel Industries B-96, Wazirpur Industrial Area Main Ring Road Delhi 110052	Steel racks
15.	Mehra & Co. 2120, Bahadurgarh Road Opp. Deputy Ganj Delhi 110006	Various library furniture and stationery items
16.	Pilco Marketing & Mfg. Co. B-96, Wazirpur Industrial Area Ring Road Delhi 110052	Steel racks

17.	Premier Library Equipment Co. 101 Nirmal Colony Near Bharat Nagar Delhi 110052	Various library furniture and stationery items
18.	Rosentique Pvt. Ltd. 503, Doctor House Pedder Road Bombay 400 026	For cubicles (carrels) designed on modular system
19.	Sardana Art Centre 87, Mohan Singh Place Connaught Place New Delhi 110001	Display racks, revolving as well as stationary types
20.	Standard Library Service 4/9 Asaf Ali Road New Delhi 110002	Various library furniture and stationery items.
21.	Trend Moulded Furniture 19, Furniture Block Kirtinagar New Delhi 110015	For chairs
22.	Trigon Metal Sections 4/15, Industrial Estate Gorwa Road, Vadodra 390 003	Steel racks

5

Central Building Research Institute (CBRI) & Its Library

The Central Building Research Institute (CBRI), Roorkee is one of the premier national laboratory amongst the thirty eighth national laboratories established by the Council of Scientific and Industrial Research (CSIR). New Delhi. It has now its own long journey, started in 1947 with as a small nucleus, called the Building Research Unit, in a couple of rooms in Thomason College of Engineering. University of Roorkee, now Indian Institute of Technology, Roorkee (IITR). The Building Research Unit was raised to the status of an institute and named as the Central Building Research Institute in 1950. On 12th April, 1953. Mr. Maulana Abul Kalam Azad, Minister of Natural Resources and Scientific Research, inaugurated the present building in the presence of Pandit Jawaharlal Nehru, Prime Minister of India. Dr. S. S. Bhatnagar. Director General. CSIR, Pandit Govind Ballabh Pant, Chief Minister of Uttar Pradesh and other dignitories.

The institute has completed more than fifty years of its existence with considerable achievements to its credit in the area of building science and technology. The major thrust areas of the institute have been:

* Shelter Planning
* New Materials
* Structure and Foundation Engineering
* Disaster Mitigation and Process Development

The Significant achievements of CBRI has a long list performed through different divisions and sections: Under the guidance of **Education and Health Buildings** division, more than 300 Navodaya Vidyalaya complexes, 616 health care buildings in Uttar Pradesh and 500 buildings were constructed. It has also set up different guidelines for barrier free built environment for physically handicapped and community health centres. **Organic Building Materials** division has developed various organic building materials like EPS door -shutters - a hundred percent wood substitute, epoxy-phenolic IPN coating etc. The **Clay Products** division has always advanced the fabrication of clay products such as, burnt clay clay-fly ash brick and tiles calcium silicate bricks and also developed high draught kiln etc. **The Environmental Science and Technology** division has promoted and contributed several products eco- friendly towards the preservation of environment. Among them lime shaft kiln, activated lime- pozzolona mixture, pollution control system for limekiln, masonary cements etc. The **Structural Engineering** division has a long tradition of being involved in the development of several structural elements viz. twin twisted reinforcing bars for steel reinforcement, design and construction methods for funicular shells, folded plates and suggested earthquake resistance measures. The **Geotechnical Engineering** has been active in landslide hazard zonation of Garwhals and Sikkim Himalayas, designed foundations for heavy storage-tanks, satellite station, dock yards towers and high rise buildings, pile foundation, reclamation of abandoned fly ash ponds for human settlements and set up strong motion seismic instrumentation etc. **The Rural Building and Environment** division has always focussed on improvement in traditional building materials and new construction techniques besides sanitation and environment technique. The **Building Process Plant and Productivity** division has developed various products which have become more popular such as pre-cast stone blocks and solid concrete block, concrete block making machine, brick extrusion machine etc. The **Efficiency of Building** division has done considerable R&D work in the assessment of solar radiation, thermal performance of building components, day lighting and natural ventilation in buildings and studied impact noise reduction in multistoried buildings etc. The **Fire Engineering division** has been in the forefront in the development of fire retardant materials and fire resistance system such as fire retardant thatch, cotton textiles and canvas, fire blocking layers, fire resistance metallic and non- metallic doors, partition and coating etc. It has also evaluated the design and commissioning of new fire evaluation facilities.

CBRI is renowned for the **consultancy** services it offers to building material construction agencies regarding all aspects of building science and technologies. It has more than 130 types of testing facilities of building materials and components as per IS, BS and ASTM Standards. This institute also maintains linkage with national and international bodies in the similar field.

CBRI LIBRARY

Library is a basic component of R & D institute. Along with

CBRI its library was established in 1947-48 to support the R&D programmes of the institute. Over the years, it has shared the challenges in achieving desired heights with its various activities. Started with the small collection in a single room now it has been grown as huge collection placed in L shape big hall on the first floor in the main building. To cop with the space problem, library has been evolved a separate section known as "Archival and Depository Section" combined the old editions (22 years back) and less use documents of main library along with the old collection of SERC library located in first floor in the building of Structural Engineering Division.

COLLECTION

The basic collection of library consists on the areas of building science and technology and its surrogate subjects. Total collection includes 59.000 (approx.) which comprises of: Books; Conference Proceedings; Technical Reports: Bound Volumes of Periodicals; Micro films; Compact Disks; Standards i.e. IS, BS, ASTM ; Reference materials and others.

INSTITUTIONAL MEMBERSHIP

The library has continued the linkage with the membership of national and international learned and professional societies and received their publications against the membership. These organizations at national level viz. Indian Academy of Science. Bangalore; Indian Building Congress. Delhi; Indian Geotechnical Society, Delhi; Indian Society of Eearthquake Technology. Rookee; Consultancy Development Centre. Delhi: Disaster Management Institute. Bhopal: Institute of Steel Development and Growth. Kolkata: Tata Energy Research Institute, Delhi; Indian Library Association, Delhi; Indian Association of Special Libraries and Information Centres, Kolkata.

Foreign organizations are: American Society for Testing Materials (ASTM), USA; International Council for Research and

Innovation in Building and Construction (CIB), The Netherlands; International Association for Housing Science (IAHS). USA; and International Union of Testing and Research Laboratories for Material and Structures, France.

Besides membership, the library received different publications in the form of annual reports, technical reports, newsletters, special serial publication etc. from various organizations in India as well as abroad.

Serial Subscription: At present library is subscribing 131 nos. of journals (76 foreign + 51 Indian) in print versions and two no. of CD - ROM's. Now nearly 1500 nos. of full text journals published from Elsevier Science and Academic Press are available on line under the banner of **www.sciencedirect.com** through CSIR E-journals Consortium.

AUTOMATION

To meet the growing requirements of the scientific community automation of the library was initiated in 1997. A network system was set up through Window NT server in Client-server environment with an integrated multi-user library management software LIBSYS. comprising of five main modules viz Acquisition, Catalouging, Circulation. Serial Control. Article Indexing and OPAC to encompass various library activities.

SERVICES

Library is playing a coordinating role between users and literature, providing personal information service CAS and SDI using information communication technology. Besides the day to day circulation. *reference* and referral services, library is providing the following prominent services:

a) Paper Clipping Service

b) Bibliographic service

c) List of latest Addition

d) CD-ROM search

e) On-line access and OPAC search

f) Xeroxing service

BIBLIOGRAPHIC DATABASE

In-house database: CBRI library has created in-house bibliographic database of the present collection of all kinds of books, standards and bound volumes and CD's are available for OPAC search.

International Construction Database (ICONDA): It is a bibliographic database compiled by CIB and produced \ marketed by Silver Platter Information. USA. It covers wide range of materials like research articles published in journals: conference proceedings: research / technical reports and technical books, standards in different languages on building science and technology. It contains data since 1976 and updated quarterly subscribed through CD - ROM.

Science Direct Navigator: It is a single bibliographic database containing over 12 million records and database from more than 7.000 scientific, technical and medical journals. It is web based on line search of Elsevier Science available in CBRI under CSIR E-journals consortium.

FULL TEXT DATABASE

Indian Standards on CD: Indian Standards on CD's brought out by Bureau of Indian Standards. Manak Bhavan. New Delhi and Produced / marketed by Book Supply Bureau. New Delhi. CBRI Library subscribes only Civil Engineering Division. It contains about 1700 Indian Standards on full text on Civil Engineering. It is updated quarterly and sent through CD's.

Annual Conference Proceedings of CIB on CD's : Other full text databases are available on CD's viz. on Indian patents. produced by NRDC, New Delhi; on Vashtushastra; Indian heritage building and monuments etc. in CBRI library.

"Library is a growing organism "is a fifth Law of library science. As a natural process rapid growth is occurred during childhood stage and it has slowed down during post-adult period. Perhaps it is true in respect of print collection only. Now the time how the library can be served in better way to the users with pin-pointed, updated information in time. Due to Information Communication Technology (ICT) and its application to library it is easy to provide variety of services without losing any time. The information can be gathered with in a few minutes using web based search at national and global level using on-line access of E-journals, E-books and of databases of other libraries. So why CBRI library has been initiated the collection of E-documents. on-line access of journals and international databases and moving towards the digital library.

6

History of the University Library

INTRODUCTION

Libraries have been called the fruits and roots of civilization. The progress and development of a country is evidenced by the number of well equipped and organised libraries it possesses. This principle holds good in the case of Educational Institutions as well. The efficiency of an educational institution can well be gauged from its Library. In other words, the growth and development of a library is in direct proportion to the teaching standard and educational attainment of the institution.

The Roorkee University, formerly known as the Thomason Engineering College established on October 19, 1847, is a world renowned institution of Technical Education. It is proud of its excellent Library with a fine collection of about 2,25,000 volumes on different branches of Engineering, Bio Science, Mathematics, Pure & Applied Sciences, Architecture, History and Art. Library subscribes to over 600 current periodicals on Engineering, Science and Humanities besides receiving about 100 periodicals as gratis or on exchange basis. In addition to the Central Library all the 18 Departments of the University maintain Departmental Libraries which are mostly Reference Libraries for meeting the special needs of faculty members and post graduate students. Its Library can be classified as one of the most well equipped Technical Libraries of the country.

A. Building

From the very start of the Institution (i.e., 1847) a small college Library was established with a collection of a few hundred books to meet the needs of about 34 students and 6 teachers. Later, in 1856 its stocks were considerably augumented by the amalgamation of the Ganges Canal Library and the College Company was added with the result that the collection of institution assumed considerable size and value.

In order to meet the growing needs of the institution, strength of which had increased from 34 students in 1847 to in 1873, a separate library block was constructed in the year 1873 comprising of two big halls, one serving as Stack Room? and the other as a Reading Room and two small side rooms behind the screen jobs.

With the many sided developments of the Thompson Engineering College and its later elevation to the rank of a University in the year 1949, the need for a separate Library Building was keenly felt. The foundation stone of the present Library Building to be called the Hafiz Mohammad Ibrahim Library (after the then, Irrigation Power & Finance Minister of (U.P.) was laid on November 25, 1949 by Pt. Govind Ballabh Pant, the then Chief Minister of U.P. The University Grants| Commission provided funds for a three storeyed Library Building to be constructed at an approximate cost of Rs. 5,00,000/- *By* 1961 the new building was almost ready and the material from] the old library was shifted to the new building. The Stack Rooms and Reading Rooms of the present building are fully air conditioned. There is provision for Seminar. Room, Research Scholar's Rooms, Cubicles, Photocopying Room, Archival] Section Hall. In order to meet the growing need of Periodical Section particularly that of additional shelving space for back

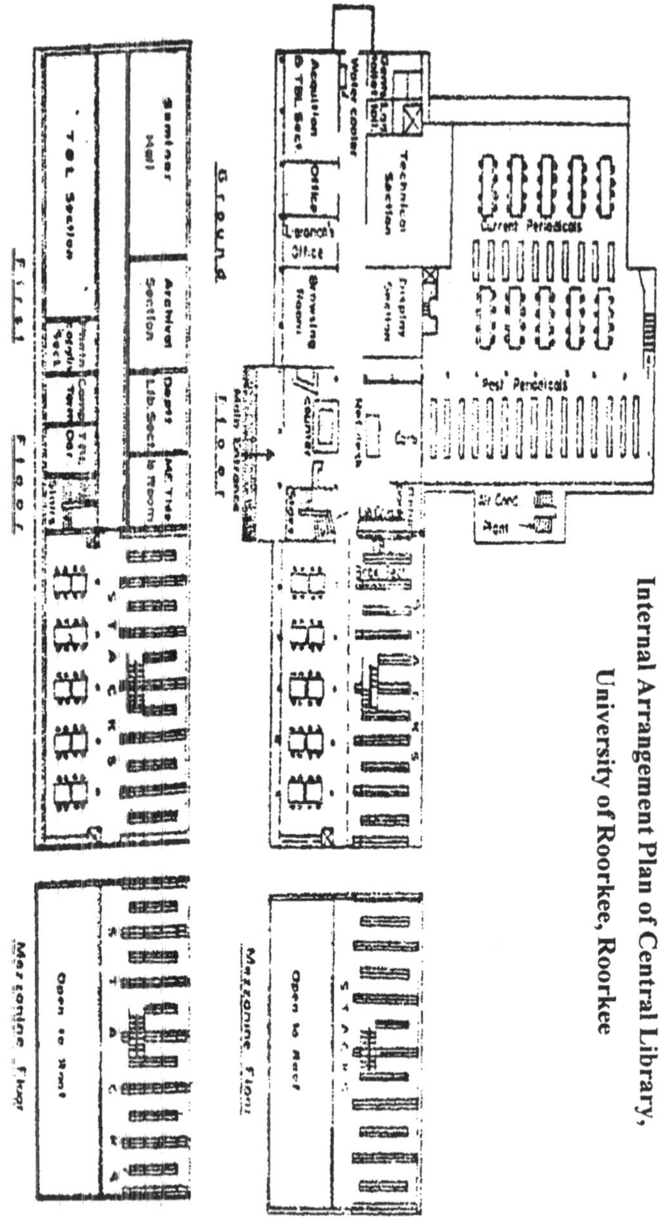

Internal Arrangement Plan of Central Library,
University of Roorkee, Roorkee

volumes of periodicals, the UGC provided a sum of Rs 3.5 lacs for construction of one reading room & one stack room above the existing area of periodical section in 1985-86.

7

Indian Institute of Technology Roorkee (Formerly University of Roorkee) At a Glance

The Institute has an illustrious history and a glorious past. It has its foundations in the Roorkee College, which was founded in 1847, to train technical manpower for making the Ganga Canal. It was the first Engineering College in the entire British Empire at that time. This was later renamed as the Thomason College of Civil Engineering in 1854. The College laid the foundation of modern engineering education and the use of civil engineering practices in the infrastructure development of the country. Major civil works in the country like dams, canals, roads, highways, railways, bridges etc., are the outcome of the engineering education imparted in this College.

In 1946. when teaching in Electrical and Mechanical Engineering was started, the college was renamed as Thomason College of Engineering. In 1949, it was elevated to the status of the first engineering University of independent India. Ever since its inception, the University has grown phenomenally in size and reach. On September 21, 2001, the University was converted to an IIT by the Government of India through an Act of Parliament, and is now known as the Indian Institute of Technology. Roorkee. The most conspicuous feature of the Institute is that the academic directions are all the time conceived to be relevant to the Indian society and its needs.

The Institute has modern education and training programmes in engineering, applied sciences and social sciences including management. The Institute has excellent lecture theatres, laboratories, libraries and computational & networking facilities. The Institute is well endowed with modern auditoria, conferencing, multi-media and video facilities and well maintained guest houses.

IIT Roorkee is situated at the foothill of the Himalayas, in Hardwar district, in the newly formed state of Uttaranchal. It is the gateway to the pilgrim centres of Hardwar, Rishikesh, Badrinath and Kedarnath. and tourist attractions of Dehradun and Mussoorie. Roorkee is well connected to Delhi by rail and road. It is situated on National Highway 58 and is on Amristar-Howrah main rail route. New Delhi -Dehradun-New Delhi Shatabdi Express and Dehradun-New Delhi-Dehradun Janshatabdi Express stop at Roorkee and make travel between Delhi and Roorkee convenient. The nearest airport is located at Jollygrant, Dehradun. However. New Delhi is the preferred airport.The Institute has two campuses; the main campus is at Roorkee in Uttaranchal and the other one is 50 km away at Saharanpur in Uttar Pradesh. The campus at Roorkee is spread over 146 hectares (356 acres) of landscaped greenery. Nestled within this are several heritage buildings, modern academic departments, hostels, messes, hospital, school, banks, community centres, playing fields, sports stadium, a modern swimming pool, yoga bhawan, dairy, students' clubs and several activity centres and other buildings. The Department of Paper Technology is located in a 10-hectare campus at Saharanpur. A new M. Tech. Programme in Information Technology was started in 2001-2002 academic session in association with Electronics Research & Development Centre India (ER&DCI) at Noida.

Co-curricular and extra-curricular activities are carried out under the auspices of the Students' Club, Hobbies Club, Cultural Society, the Himalayan Explorers' Club, Educational Cinema Club, Sports Association, National Cadet Corps (NCC) and various departmental students' societies. The National Assessment and Accreditation Council (NACC), under the UGC, has given the highest rating, five star, to the erstwhile University of Roorkee.

ACADEMIC DEPARTMENTS AND CENTRES

The Institute is one of the biggest technical institutions in the country, with the largest number of academic units. It has 18 academic departments covering engineering, applied sciences, humanities & social sciences, and management programmes, 6 centres and large number of research centres.

Academic Departments

* Architecture & Planning
* Bio-Technology
* Chemical Engineering
* Chemistry
* Civil Engineering
* Earth Sciences
* Earthquake Engineering
* Electrical Engineering

* Electronics & Computer Engineering
* Humanities & Social Sciences
* Hydrology
* Management Studies
* Mathematics
* Mechanical & Industrial Engineering
* Metallurgical & Materials Engineering
* Paper Technology
* Physics
* Water Resource Development Training Centre

Centres

* Alternate Hydro Energy Centre
* Institute Instrumentation Centre
* Centre for Continuing Education
* Information Superhighway Centre
* Institute Computer Centre
* Quality Improvement Programme Centre

TEACHING AND EVALUATION SYSTEM

Each academic year is divided into two semesters and teaching programmes are organized around the credit system. Teaching includes lectures, tutorials, practicals, projects, seminars, dissertations, and field & industrial training. The Institute lays special emphasis on the tutorial system, which is based on a close personal interaction between students and teachers. The undergraduate students have to undergo a comprehensive project during the final year of their studies. A distinct feature of the education system at Roorkee is the emphasis on overall personality development and instilling in students the qualities of leadership. Thus, extra curricular activities are an important part of student life. The Institute has provided the largest number of engineers in the task of nation building.

Academic committees and faculty board of each Department use course-appraisal to review the course content. At the end of each semester every student gives a feedback on the course content, its relevance and performance of the teacher. Teachers, for maintaining continuity of the course, also maintain course files. Feed back from students has helped in continually improving courses and teaching quality.

ACADEMIC STATISTICS FOR 2001 -2002

Staff Strength

Academic Staff	355
Administrative & Supporting Staff	1288
	Total 1643

Student Strength

Undergraduate (UG) Programmes	1639
Postgraduate (PG) Programmes	1373
Ph.D.	281
	Total 3293

Students/Academic Staff Ratio =9.27:1

PG/UG Students Ratio = 1:1

Number of Students Admitted

Ph.D.	53
M. Phil	25
M. Tech.	358
M.Arch./MURP	12
M. Sc.	179
M.B.A.	60
M.C.A.	30
PG Diploma	55

B.Tech.	382
B.Arch.	37
	Total 1191

ACADEMIC PROGRAMMES

IIT Roorkee offers a wide range of academic programmes. It runs 10 undergraduate, 55 postgraduate and several doctoral programmes. **3293** students were studying in different programmes in the session 2001-2002.

Undergraduate (UG) Programmes

The Institute offers ten undergraduate programmes leading to B. Arch and B. Tech. degrees, which are of 5 and 4 years duration, respectively. These programmes are:

Architecture

Chemical Engineering

Civil Engineering

Computer Science & Engineering

Electrical Engineering

Electronics & Communication Engineering

Industrial Engineering

Mechanical Engineering

Metallurgical Engineering

Pulp and Paper Engineering

During the session 2001-2002, **419** students were admitted to different UG programmes and a total of **1639** were registered in different years of UG programmes. All the IITs make admission to these programmes on the basis of a Joint Entrance Examination (J.E.E.).

Postgraduate (PG) Programmes

The predecessor of the IIT Roorkee, the University of Roorkee, pioneered postgraduate programmes in engineering and technology, way back in 1955. During the session 2001-2002, 719 students were admitted to the PG programmes and a total of 1373 students were registered in these programmes.

Admission to PG programmes is made on the basis of GATE score and/or on the basis of the written test and interviews. Non Resident Indians (NRI) and foreign nationals are also admitted to PG programmes. Sponsored candidates, including those through Quality Improvement Programme (QIP), form another channel for admissions to these programmes. IIT Roorkee is the only institution in the country having specialized PG programmes in Earthquake Engineering, Water Resources Development & Management, Hydrology, Welding Engineering, Alternate Hydro Energy and Pulp and Paper Technology.

Doctoral Programmes

Research programmes leading to the degree of Doctor of Philosophy (Ph.D.) are available in all academic departments of the Institute. While 53 new candidates were admitted to Ph.D. programme, a total of 281 candidates were working for their Ph.D. degree in the session 2001-2002. The Ph.D. thesis is evaluated by the supervisor(s) who is the internal examiner(s) and by two external examiners, one Indian and the other from abroad. If the examiners recommend acceptance of the thesis, a viva voce examination of the candidate is arranged at Roorkee. The recommendations of the Board of Examiners are considered by the Senate, which approves the award of Ph.D. degree to the candidate.

CONTINUING EDUCATION PROGRAMMES

Centre for Continuing Education

The Centre for Continuing Education acts as a window to disseminate knowledge of latest technological developments. The Centre organizes short-term programmes to meet the growing needs of both private and public sector organisations. These programmes include the ones sponsored by the industry and government organisations for the benefit of their own engineers & personnel as also the ones conducted by the Institute. The Centre has so far conducted approximately 1100 training programmes, for over 15,000 engineers, scientists and technocrats from India and abroad.

The Ministry of Human Resources Development (MHRD) has selected this Centre as one of the nodal agencies for preparing self-study packages in various areas for working professionals. This project is now funded by the AICTE and the centre has prepared 80 packages.

Quality Improvement Programme Centre

The Government of India launched the Quality Improvement Programme (QIP) in 1971 to upgrade the expertise and capabilities of faculty members of degree level engineering institutions in the country.

The three principal activities of the Centre are: Providing opportunities to technical faculty members of recognised degree level engineering institutions to improve their qualifications (Masters and Ph.D. programmes); organizing short-term courses (STCs) for serving teachers; and curriculum development and any other activity to help improve the standards of technical education.

Development of educational material is based on modern education technology such as multimedia teaching aids, computer based instructional packages, audio-visual material, video films, books, monographs, laboratory manuals etc.

The Institute is a host institution, under the AICTE's Early Faculty Induction Programme (EFIP), and attracts young faculty in areas facing shortage of teachers.

SCHOLARSHIPS, PRIZES AND FINANCIAL ASSISTANCE

The Institute offers merit-cum-means scholarship to 25%

of undergraduate students. Several other scholarships are announced from time to time. Other facilities are also provided to undergraduate students in the shape of Institute free studentship, scholarship to students belonging to the scheduled castes and scheduled tribes. Students admitted to the 2-year M.Sc. *degree* in sciences are also awarded merit-cum-means scholarships.

A number of scholarships, teaching/research assistantship schemes provide financial support to students of M.Tech. and Ph.D. programmes. Sponsored (full-time as well as part-time) self-financing foreign students and M.B.A. students are, however, not eligible for benefits of this scheme. Avenues are also available to the students to earn while they learn. Prizes and certificates are given to students on the basis of their performance in curricular, co-curricular and extra curricular activities.

PROFESSORIAL CHAIRS

The Institute encourages companies and government and other organisations to establish Professorial Chairs in the emerging and relevant areas of engineering, science, technology, humanities & social sciences including management studies. Brief particulars of some chairs currently occupied in the Institute are given below:

Indian Railways Chairs

Two Professorial Chairs, one in the area of Bridge Engineering and the other in the area of Dynamics of Rail Vehicle Systems, have been instituted by Indian Railways. The scope of work includes R & D, dissemination of knowledge, human resource development, advice to Railways on specific projects related to the chair and coordination of activities with other railway organisations such as Research, Development and Standardization Organisation (RDSO).

The thrust areas in Bridge Engineering include health monitoring and rehabilitation of existing old bridges, rationalization and modernization of design specification and codes, field investigations of bridge, studies related to scour etc.

Areas of activity in Dynamics of Rail Vehicle Systems include rail wheel interaction, track irregularities, hunting and lateral stability, vertical dynamics and side behaviour, and performance and dynamics of over-head transmission lines.

Pandit G.B. Pant Chair

During the birth centenary celebrations of Pandit G.B. Pant in 1987-88, the U.P. Government instituted a Professorial Chair, which has been named as "Pt. Govind Ballabh Pant Professorial Chair in Environmental Pollution Abatement". The awardee of the Chair is placed in one of the academic departments of the Institute depending on the work plan of the Chair Professor.

MEMORANDA OF UNDERSTANDING/ COLLABORATIVE PROGRAMMES

Indian Institute of Technology Roorkee encourages active involvement of faculty and students in collaborative programmes at national and international level in order to remain at the forefront of the scientific and technological development and to share its experience with them.

In order to have close cooperation in the field of teaching and research the Senate and the Board of Governors of IIT Roorkee have approved MoUs with:

1. **University of Waterloo, Canada**

   * Academic development including academic programmes and student training.
   * Research projects preferably of a collaborative nature involving scholars from University of Waterloo and Indian Institute of Technology Roorkee.
   * Exchange of scholars for appropriate periods of time.
   * Development and exchange of publications, data and other teaching materials.

2. Kungl Tekniska Hogskolan, (Kth), Stockholm, Sweden

* Cooperation between research groups, researchers and Institute faculty and exchange visits for teaching and research.

3. Government of Uttaranchal, Dehradun

* Strategic partnership to launch IT initiatives in the State in the fields of e-Governance, e-Education, Telemedicine, GIS and other related fields.

4. Department of Atomic Engineering, Mumbai

* To establish the Institute Training Scheme of the Department of Atomic Energy (DAE) in various engineering disciplines and to make available additional sources of trained manpower for pursuing various activities of DAE at the national level.

INTERNATIONAL COOPERATION

The Institute has played a very important role in international cooperation, particularly for developing countries, in the field of engineering, applied sciences and social sciences including management education. It attracts a very large number of students from over 50 countries. Water Resources Development Training Centre (WRDTC) and the Department of Hydrology run special post graduate (PG) programmes for students of Afro Asian region. The Institute has awarded undergraduate degrees after 4 year of study on the campus to special groups of students from Tanzania, Ethiopia, Lesotho and Nepal.

Admission of foreign nationals to various Postgraduate and Research Programmes is made through the following channels:

* Indian Council of Cultural Research (ICCR)
* Technical Cooperation Service of Colombo Plan
* Indian Technology Research Services
* UNESCO
* World Meteorological Organisation

FACULTY AND ALUMNI DISTINCTIONS

The faculty and alumni of the Institute have contributed handsomely in the development of the nation. They have also earned a good name for themselves worldwide. Some important distinctions, awards and honours bestowed on them are as given below:

Eight of our faculty members/alumni have been recipients of the prestigious Padma Vibhsuhan, Padma Bhushan and Padma Shree awards. The latest addition to this glorious list is the award of Padma Bhushan to the Chairman Board of Governors, IIT Roorkee, Prof. S.K. Joshi in 2003. Over the years, 7 have been honoured with the prestigious S.S. Bhatnagar award. More than 100 have been bestowed with top level appointments such as - Governor, Director General of Council for Scientific and Industrial Research (CSIR), Secretary Government of India (or equivalent), members of Union Public Service Commission, Chairman of All India Council for Technical Education (AICTE) and likes; Vice Chairman of (UGC), Chairman of (CWC), Chairman of Railway Board, Directors of IITs/Vice-Chancellors/Directors of R&D Institutes. A large number of Alumni have been Chief Engineers & Head of various State & Central Government Organisations like State PWD, Central PWD, State Electrical Boards, Irrigation Departments, etc. Prof. S.K. Joshi, Chairman Board of Governers of IIT Roorkee, (and former Director General Council of Scientific & Industrial Research (CSIR), and Professor & Head of Department of Physics of University of Roorkee) has been awarded the Padma Bhushan in the honours list of Republic day, 2003.

Four faculty members and alumni have been presidents of national academies and professional institutions, and more than 25 are fellows of National Academies like Indian National Science Academy (INSA) and Indian National Academy of Engineering (INAE).

ALUMNI ACTIVITIES

Professor In Charge Alumni Affairs

The Office of Professor-In-Charge, Alumni Affairs has been created to establish a direct link between the alumni and the institute. An Advisory Committee advises the Professor-In-Charge on its activities, which include:

* Promotion of network with the alumni
* Promoting the role of alumni in institute's programmes and activities
* Receiving funds/donations for the Institute directly from the alumni
* Creating a platform for exchange of ideas and views among alumni
* Any other activity considered desirable for development of the institute and for creating goodwill among alumni.

Thomason Alumni Association

The alumni association of the institute called The Thomason Alumni Association (formerly the Roorkee University Alumni Association) strives to promote and encourage members to take active interest in the activities and progress of the alma mater. Other objectives are

* To award scholarships and financial aid to students.
* To help create better residential, educational and recreational facilities for the Institute community.
* To promote and encourage friendly relations between all members of the association.
* To keep the alumni informed about the alma mater.
* To exchange professional knowledge.

The Association publishes a quarterly newsletter called "Thomasonian" through which it disseminates news of the alma mater and the Alumni. The Association also has a website, "eroorkee.com", for easy and fast interaction amongst the alumni. At present the association has over fourteen thousand members and has *35* local chapters in India, USA and Kuwait.

SPONSORED RESEARCH AND INDUSTRIAL CONSULTANCY

The Institute encourages faculty members to undertake research projects in frontier areas of engineering, science, technology and management. Major funding has been attracted from government agencies like Ministries of Science and Technology, Communication and Information Technology, Non-Conventional Energy Sources, Environment & Forest and Surface Transportation of Government of India, CSIR, ISRO, CWC, DRDO and DAE.

The Institute extends benefit of research and development to the country's industrial and economic growth in the form of consultancy services. This provides a first hand knowledge of current problems in the industry and is used in fine-tuning the curriculum to meet the emerging national challenges and needs. The Institute, through its faculty, can handle almost any type of problem/need of the industry. An illustrative list of the types of consultancy services currently being offered is given below:

* Analytical studies
* Cause-and-remedy studies
* Pre-feasibility and feasibility studies
* Detailed project reports
* Design of systems/components/processes
* Validation of designs/drawings
* Development of industrial products/systems/processes
* Development of systems software
* Development of application software for offline and online applications

* Testing of industrial products/samples
* Residual-life assessment of plants and equipments
* Calibration of sensors and instruments
* Development of laboratories
* Self/distance learning multi-media packages

Administrative and accounting support to the faculty undertaking sponsored research and consultancy work is provided by a full-fledged office operating under Dean, Sponsored Research and Industrial Consultancy (SRIC).

PLACEMENT SERVICES

The Institute provides placement opportunities to students through on-campus recruitment organized by the Professor Placement, Training and Industrial Liaison under the umbrella of the Dean Sponsored Research and Industrial Consultancy (SRIC). The Institute has an excellent track record of placement of students in spite of the economic slowdown in the current year.

SUPPORT SERVICES

The Institute's support services include the library, computing, networking and medical services.

Libraries

The Institute's Central Library is one of the biggest libraries for engineering and technology education in the country. This heritage library has manuscripts, books and journals of historical and archival importance, and also houses the latest science and engineering journals. In addition, each academic department has a reference library of moderate size.

Institute Computer Centre (ICC)

The Institute has excellent computing facilities. The Institute Computer Centre has TATA ELX1 and PARAM 10000 Super

Computers, SG Workstation, along with a large number of PCs, printers etc.

Information Super Highway Centre (ISC)

The Centre provides Internet and Intranet services to the staff and students with a bandwidth of 2 Mbps from BSNL and 512 Kbps SCPC from ERNET.

Medical Services

The Institute has a well-equipped 60-bed hospital in Roorkee campus. The hospital provides medical services to the Institute staff, their dependents and students. Some of the facilities available are x-ray, physiotherapy, diathermy, ECG, pathological testing, blood analyser and ultrasound. The Saharanpur campus has another hospital of moderate size to serve the students, staff and families residing there.

STUDENTS' GUIDE TO THE LIBRARY

LIBRARY HOURS

Monday through Friday	8.30a.m. to 10.00p.m.
Saturday/Sunday/Holiday	9.45 a.m. to 6.30 p.m.
Winter & Summer Vacation	10.00 a.m. to 6.30 p.m.

1.2 The library will remain open on all days except on the following holidays.

Republic Day

Holi-2 days

Idul-Fitr

Janmashtmi

Shivratri

Independence day

Dushera

Mahatma Gandhi Birthday

Christmas

2. MEMBERSHIP

All students and research scholars are eligible to become member of the Library. Application for membership should be made on the prescribed form available from information section.

3. ADMISSION TO THE LIBRARY

Before entering the Library, the gate register is to be signed and the Identity card shown at the entry point. Private books, bags, cases, personal effects and printed matter other than library books must not be brought inside the library. These should be deposited at the property counter. Library does not accept any responsibility for loss or damage to personal property left on its premises.

4. LOAN PRIVILEGE

Research Scholars & : P. G. Students	5 books/documents for 14 days loan
	1 book/document for overnight loan
U.G. Students :	3 books/documents for 14 days loan
	1 book/document for overnight loan

5. HOW TO SEARCH A BOOK IN THE LIBRARY

Central Library maintains catalogue of all the documents held by it. This catalogue is available in print from as well as On-line Catalogue.

5.1 Manual Catalogue

The manual catalogue is comprised of two parts i.e. the Author and the Subject Catalogue. The entries in Author Catalogue are arranged according to surname of the author in alphabetical order. The entries in Subject Catalogue are arranged according to subjects in alphabetical order. User can search the document through Author's name or through subject/keyword,

5.2 On-line Catalogue

It is available on Intranet of the institute. By inputting http://192.168.125.20 in the browser (i.e. Internet Explorer or Netscape Navigator) the library homepage is opened. There are various options on this page, By clicking the search option, search page is opened. You can search a book by author, title or accession number, Detailed help is available on the website itself. In case of any difficulty library personnel may be contacted for assistance.

6. CIRCULATION SECTION

The Circulation Section will remain open between 10.30 a.m. to 7.00 p.m. on weekdays. On Saturdays/Sundays and holidays only reading rooms and periodical section will remain open. There will be no issue and return of books/jls. on these days.

	ISSUE HOURS	*RETURN HOURS*
General books	10.30 a.m.-7.00 p.m.	10.30 a.m.-7.00 p.m.
Text books and Reference books for consultation inside the library	8.30 a.m.-10.00 p.m.	
Text books (overnight issue)	5.00p.m. - 7.00p.m.	9.00a.m. - 1.00p.m.
Loose and bound Journals	5.00p.m.-7.00p.m.	9.00a.m. - 1.00p.m.

7. ISSUE SYSTEM

Books shall be issued on the presentation of identity card and Library ticket.

7.1 Library tickets are non transferable. These will be valid for the duration of the academic session for which these are issued.

7.2 Before leaving the issue counter, the member should satisfy that the books lent to him/her are in a sound condition and if not he/she shall immediately bring the matter to the notice of the officer on duty. If a book is returned in damaged condition the borrower will be held responsible for its replacement by a sound copy.

7.3 Books and journals issued to members should be got checked and issue token returned to the attendant at the check point.

8. TICKETS & TOKEN

8.1 Tickets should be renewed in the beginning of every academic year. For this old tickets and registration card should be presented at the Circulation desk.

8.2 In case the reader's tickets get mutilated because of use or other wise, it must be reported to the Library. Under no condition these should be over written.

8.3 Special care should be taken so that reader's tickets and property token are not misplaced or lost. Tickets are non transferable. All losses are to be reported immediately to the Librarian.

9. OVERDUES & FINES

9.1 If book is not returned on due date, an overdue fine of Rs. 1.00 per volume per day is levied. Books and Journals issued for overnight loan should be returned on the next day by 1.00 p.m. after.that a fine of Rs. 5.00 per volume per day shall be charged of non return of such material.

10. RESERVATION AND TRACING OF BOOKS

Timings : 7.30 pm to 8.30 pm

10.1 Book reservation will be made out of the books returned on a particular date. Students will be required to note the desired book in the reservation register kept with the Duty Officer10.2

If a book is not traceable by a student, he may apply for its search. For this he should fill SEARCH CARD and handover to the Duty Officer for further action.

11. TEXT BOOK LOAN SCHEME/BOOK BANK

This section exclusively contains 36,000 (approx.) recent editions of text books prescribed for study at the undergraduate and M.Sc/M.Tech.(Earth Sciences) level. A student may become member of the scheme on payment of prescribed fee. One may get three text books issued for semester duration. Text books may be exchanged on all working Tuesdays and Fridays. A fine of Rs. 1.00 per volume per day shall be charged after the last date of returned is over. For rules and procedure, contact the Head, TBL Scheme/Book Bank scheme.

12. DEPARTMENTAL LIBRARIES

Every teaching department has its own Library. Students are advised to contact O.C. Library for rules for use of departmental libraries.

13. RESEARCH REFERENCE & INFORMATION SERVICES

This section contains research & reference tool such as Atlases, Bibliographies, Biographical dictionaries, Data books, Dictionaries (General & Special), Directories, Encyclopedias, Gazetteers, Guides to literature, Handbooks, Maps, thesauri etc. All queries about research problems and scientific information should be addressed to this section. All queries regarding admissions to Foreign Universities/ Institution and competition books can be have from foreign institution shelf.

14. CARE OF BOOKS

No person shall write upon, damage or make doddles on Library books and Journals. He shall be held responsible for any damage or injury done by him to the books, journals or any other property of the Library and shall be required to pay the penalty which may include deduction of marks from the general group of marks or other disciplinary action as the Institute may deem fit.

14.1 In case of loss of a book, the borrower will be required either to replace the book by its latest edition or pay prevailing publisher's price together with a penalty equal to the cost of the books plus overdue charges, if any. In case of rare or out of print book, the penalty may be equal to cost of reproduction of the book.

8

Central Library Indian Institute of Technology Roorkee - A Profile

'From vast print collections to thousands of online texts, from rare books to worldwide networks and interactive telecommunications, the Library is more than a rich resources-it is a service with a first rate staff committed to helping patrons tap the full potential of information resources.... '

Central Library of the Indian Institute of Technology Roorkee (formerly University of Roorkee) was established in 1848 as College Library of then College of Civil Engineering Roorkee (renamed as Thomason College of Civil Engineering Roorkee in 1854). The collections of Ganga Canal library was merged with the college library in 1850s and the library was renamed as Central Library in 1856. During 1862 the entire collection of Adiscombe College London Library was also merged with it. This is one of the oldest Academic/technical libraries of the country. The Library is a state of art library having all latest facilities like LAN integrated with the Institute Fiber Optic Network, CD-ROM Network, On-line Catalogue & Internet facilities etc. All the digital resources of the library are available on campus wide network

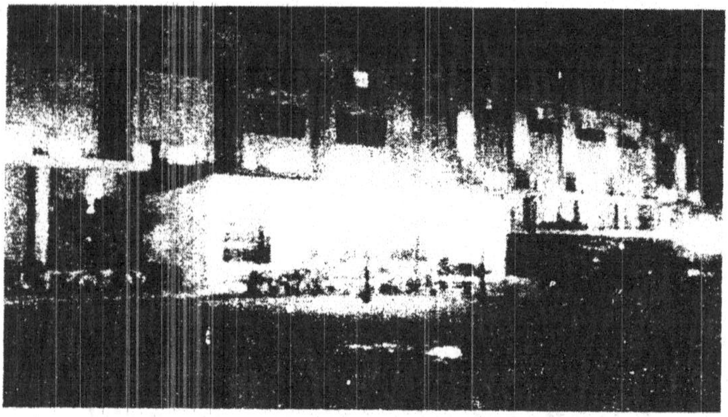

1. Library Vision

To achieve recognition as a leading educational library, which actively contributes to the achievement of Institute's vision.

2. Objectives

The Central Library is aiming to disrobe, make available and facilitate access to a broad spectrum of information resources and services to support the teaching, learning and research activities of the Institute. The library collections and services and the ways in which they are made available will complement the Institute commitment to creativity, innovation and excellence. The Central Library's objectives are:

(i) To provide universal, easy, cost-effective access to library collections and information services for every student faculty and staff members.

(ii) To provide a core collection of digital information resources through inter-institutional agreements in order to enhance learning, teaching, research and public service.

(iii) To enhance the efficiency of resource sharing among participating institutions by utilizing emerging technologies.

(iv) To provide electronic indexes, abstracts and full text of a core collection of academic journal publications.

(v) To go for cooperative acquisition process with other IITs

(vi) To have /develop centralised cataloging process in IITs

(vii) To develop a network of all IITs in collaboration with other IITs

3. Librarians of the Central Library

Till 1870 the Central Library was being managed by the College teachers as their additional assignments. In 1870 James Adversely took charge as the first full time Librarian. Since then the Library was never without a full time Librarian except a small spell during 1929. The first Indian appointed to the post was Mr. Prem Narain Sharma during 1938. After Independence the status of the Librarian was also raised and the first Librarian. The following table gives the names of Officers-in-Charge and their tenure if it was more than a year.

Year	Name	Designation
1870-1874	Sgt J.E. Aldersly	Asstt. Librarian
1875-1881	Mr. S.B. Simons	Asstt. Librarian
1882	Mr. C.C.Sullinani Aldersly	Asstt. Librarian
1882-1893	Mr: T.H.Butlor	Asstt: Librarian
1893-1898	Mr. Mr. J.H. Mee	Asstt. Librarian
1898-1900	Hony. Lt: R. Giltrap	Asstt. Librarian
1900-1908	Hony. Lt. C. Charter	Asstt. Librarian
1908-1916	Mr. H. Robey	Librarian
1917-1920	Mr. R.H. Cumming	Librarian
1921-1922	Miss E. Linsley	Librarian
1923-1928	Mr. R. Parkinaeri	Librarian
1929-		
1930-1937	Mr. J.H.Kelly	Librarian
1938-1939	Mr. Prem Narain Sharma	Librarian

1940-1943	Mr. M.I. Ansari	Librarian
1944-1945	Mr. M.M.Rafique	Librarian
1946-1949	Mr. Gyan Prakash Goel	Librarian
1949-1953	Mr. M.I.Ansari	Librarian
1953-1961	Mr. D. Gupta	Librarian
1961-1988	Mr. R.S.Saxena	Librarian
1988-1995	Mr. M.S.Rana	Librarian
1995-1996	Mr. S.P.Singh (Officiating)	Asstt. Librarian
1996 -	Mr. Yogendra Singh	Librarian

4. General Layout

Presently the Central Library is housed in a L-shape building which was constructed during 1950s. The importance given to the library since beginning is evident from the fact it was designed as a centrally air conditioned building getting the status of first air conditioned university library building in the country. It has around 5000 sq.m of floor area.

Immediately after entering the building one sees a spacious hall on the left side of which is the Reference Book Section which houses a very rich collection of reference books. Librarian's office and the New Arrival Display area is also on the left side at ground floor. On the right hand side are the Circulation Counters and main book section. Book Section has two reading halls and four book stacks floors. The ground floor houses the books on engineering, which is continued on first mezzanine floor. Books on sciences are stacked on first mezzanine. First main floor houses remaining sciences and Hindi collection while the Second mezzanine houses social sciences, humanities and architecture.

Entrance to the periodical section is on the ground floor just opposite to the main gate. The Periodical Section occupies three floors. The current journals display, reading room and the back volumes of 1983 onwards are on the ground floor. First floor houses the back volumes from 1970 to 1982. Back volumes prior to 1970 are housed on the Second floor. Second floor in this wing also houses the Text Books section. Dissertation section and dormitory where less used books are housed on third.

Just above the *reference* hall and Librarian's office is used for Acquisition and Technical Section and Archival Section. This wing also houses Server Room and Cyber Room.

5. Library Resources

5.1 Information Resources (Collection)

Being as one of the oldest technical library in India, the pride of this library is its archival and extensive collection. Its collection is unique in itself, having the possession of 18th &19th century published rare and out-of-print documents to the latest digitized from of information resources, tools and techniques. Its collection is especially strong in sciences and engineering however humanities and social science have got due attention. The total collection of books & journals is 3.00 lacs of documents out of which 46,000 are bound volumes of Journals, 12,000 archival collection 11,000 dissertations, 1500 thesis, 450 videos and 400 CDs/floppies.

5.2 Staff

Competent, skilled & dynamic staffs are backbone of any organization. Library Staff are bridge between the information resources and their users (Library members). The promptness, effectiveness and efficiency in services is need of the hour that requires technically skilled and competent staff. Central Library is trying to do so with its 43 staff out of which 23 are professionally qualified, while rest is not skill enough. Even if the Central Library has managed to run it's services in better way by their in house training. But they need some more incentives and proper training. Whatever Central Library has achieved it is its staff dedication and hard labour.

5.3 Finance

Finance is most important factor that affects the organizations activities. It can run the institute or paralyse it. The total activities and services are dependent on proper finance. Lack of financial resources was the main bottlenecks in progress of the library. UGC and state government were the main sources of finance in last years, from which library did not get sufficient funds which had affected its growth too. After becoming an IIT Library the situation has changed. Last year's total Plan and Non-plan budget was Rs. 6.00 crores.

5.4 Hardware/Software

Central Library has 54 computers including four server, 11 printers, 3 network data switch, 5 networking hubs, 6 barcode scanner,2 CD-ROM server & drives, Library Management Software, Window NT server, Office automation software etc. All these resources are the part of the Library Local Area Network(LAN) which is based on star topology. The various resources are connected through three 24 port data switches with 100 mpbs capacity. Cat5 cables and AT&T colour scheme is used for connectivity purpose. A conceptual view of Library LAN is given in the figure below.

6. Sections and their Responsibilities

6.1 Acquisition

Acquisition section deals with the selection, ordering and acquisition of books. This section does the allocation of plan and non-plan grant in different heads. The acquisition process is centralized one and documentary records for departmental purchase is systematically maintained. The activities are fully computerized except the Accession Register for audit purpose.

6.2 Technical Section

Technical section deals with the technical processing of the

CENTRAL LIBRARY NETWORK

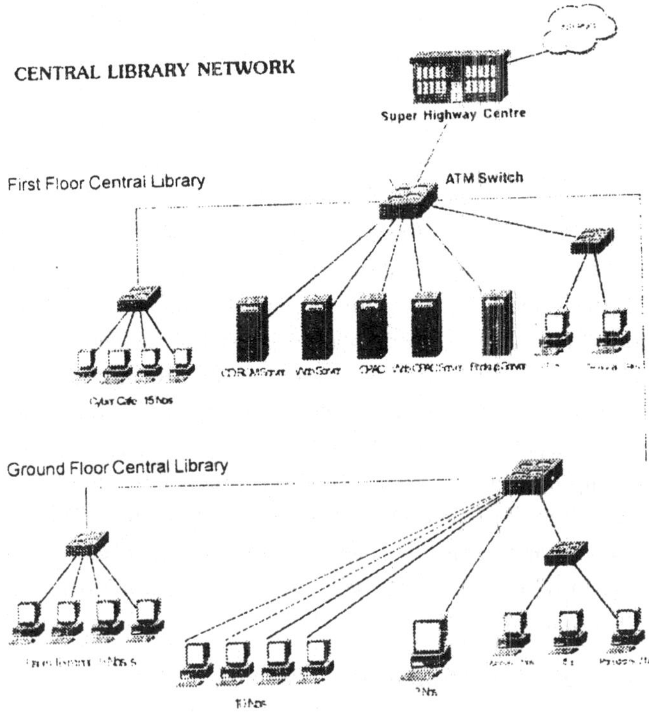

documents purchased and accessioned by acquisition section: The technical processing (classification and cataloguing) is also centralized i.e. Departmental Libraries books are also classified and catalogued here. Since we are also maintaining the manual catalogue, the catalogue cards are printed for Central Library and Departmental Libraries with our Library Software. The section activities are now fully computerized. Around 12.000 cards are prepared annually from 4000 records.

6.3 Circulation Section

Circulation section deals with registration of library members, circulation (issue/return) and consultation of books. From issue, card filing, overdue posting to return. fine posting, reservation all the activities and services are being performed through computerized system. Central Library is currently serving around 3900 members. Central Library issues around 80,000 books annually.

6.4 Periodical Section

The heart of any library is its Periodical Section. Journals are lifeblood of all R & D activities, which brings nascent thoughts to the professional community. About 70-to90% of total library budget is being spent on journals (Table -). This section deals with allocating the grant for core journals and department journals requirement. Vendor Registration, Selection of Jls. calling quotations, ordering, receipts, Kardex generation, non-receipt reminders, receiving bills and their verification, sending drafts to the selected vendors as advance payment. The next step to send reminders for non-supply, missing issues, sending credit note, binding and accessioning of bound volumes. Presently the total collection of journals is approximately **46,000** bound volumes and **650** currently subscribed Beside print Central Library also subscribe to more than 4000 e-journals.

6.5 Text Book Loan Scheme (TBLS)

TBLS section especially meant to serve the B.Tech and all M Sc/ M Tech (Earth Science) classes. This section registeres the students for a semester on fee basis. The UG and M Sc students are entitled to get three books for one semester duration. The textbooks collection has grown up to 36.000 volumes serving around 2800 students.

6.6 Automation and Networking section

The main thrust of Central Library remained on expansion of digital and electronic services besides developing the core collection of books and journals. The Central Library is marching ahead towards total automation of its services. This section is charged with total responsibility of maintenance of hardware and software and also networking.

6.7 *Archival Section*

The Archival Cell contains over 12,000 rare and out-of-print books published in the 18th and 19th centuries. The following three sub-sections are the heart of our collection:

6.7.1 *Thomason Collection Publication*

This section includes all books published by the College during the years 1847-1947. Some important books in this section include copiously produced college calendars, the world famous Roorkee Treatises, Roorkee Manuals, and some class notes in manuscript form by eminent teachers of the Thomason College, etc.

6.7.2 *The Ganges Canal Collection*

It is another important collection of all works concerning the design and construction of the Ganga Canal.

6.7.3 *Proby T. Cautley Collection*

It contains classical works by Cautley on the design and construction of the Ganga Canal, such as Report on the Ganga Canal Works: from the commencement until the opening of the Canal in 1854. This report is in three volumes. Notes and memoranda on the Eastern Jamuna or Doab Canal, on the water courses in Dehradun, sketches on the Doab Canal and Works, and Ganges Canal: Disquisition on the Heads of the Ganges and Jamuna Canal are some other works.

It was Cautley's Report Vol 2 that established the fact that first steam locomotive was used between Roorkee and Piran Kleer (small place 6 km from Roorkee) for Ganga Canal work on 22nd December 1851 well before it was used between Bombay V.T. and Thane on 16th April 1853.

7. Specialised Information Services

Besides conventional library services the Central Library provides following specialized services

7.1 On-line Public Access Catalogue

The Central Library maintains two types of on-line catalogues traditional as well as web based. Traditional catalogue has the facility of simple search, expert search as well as multilingual search with boolean combination of few fields. Web OPAC has the facility of title/key word search, author, search, accession number search and call number search. It is also possible to access the loan record of a member with proper authentication through Web OPAC. Besides this it also provides linkage to various search engines and e-resources portal.